ACKNOWLEDGMENTS

I want to thank my many friends and associates who, through their knowledge and judgment, have helped me to write this book.

In particular I gratefully acknowledge my debt to Miss Alison Outhwaite for her expert advice on the Nazi and Communist sections, Mr. Donald McLachlan for his able comment on the arrangement, and Mrs. Mark Abrams who read the proofs for me.

I have received most generous assistance from the Photographic Section of the Department of the Army at the Pentagon and the Photographic Section of the Department of the Navy at Anacostia, who have allowed me to make a selection from their fine stock and given me permission to publish it. Also the Imperial War Museum Library and the Imperial War Museum Photographs Library have been very helpful.

Lastly I thank my family and pay tribute to the hard work they have all put into the book. My husband and youngest son have read and re-read every word with patience and frank criticism.

I could not have produced the American edition without the enthusiasm and sound advice of Charles and Christine Stiassni. I am very grateful.

COVER PHOTO: UPI

By The Same Author:

People and Power: The Story of Three Nations
The Story of Africa: South of the Sahara
The Story of the United Nations

CONTENTS

"Remember Pearl Harbor"

At 7:55 A.M. on Sunday, December 7, 1941, the United States Pacific Fleet rode proudly at anchor at the Hawaiian Island base of Pearl Harbor. In "Battleship Row" there was a stately array, and on the surrounding airfields the aircraft lay in gleaming rows, wing tip to wing tip.

By 9:45 the same morning the mighty fleet and well-stocked airfields had been reduced to a mass of blackened, smoking metal.

Out of a clear sky on this quiet Sunday morning, three hundred and fifty Japanese bombers attacked without warning, leaving in their wake a shambles of death and destruction. In less than two hours the mastery of the Pacific had passed from American to Japanese hands.

The news struck America like a thunderclap. It

reached people on Sunday afternoon, broadcast from every radio station. Families were busy planning for Christmas. Now, with sickening certainty, everyone knew that life had changed. In the morning they had looked forward to the New Year; now, in the afternoon, they could only look forward to partings, sorrow, and anxiety.

In Washington on the following day President Roosevelt drove through streets lined with waiting crowds to ask Congress for a formal declaration of war against Japan. He spoke with deep conviction and quiet certainty:

Yesterday, December 7, 1941 — a date which will live in infamy — the United States of America was suddenly and deliberately attacked by naval and air forces of the Empire of Japan. . . . No matter how long it may take us to overcome this premeditated invasion, the American people, in their righteous might, will win through to absolute victory. . . . Hostilities exist. There is no blinking the fact that our people, our territory, and our interests are in grave danger. . . . With confidence in our armed forces, with the unbounding determination of our people, we will gain the inevitable triumph. So help us God. I ask that Congress declare that since the unprovoked, dastardly attack by Japan on Sunday, December 7, 1941, a state of war has existed between the United States and the Japanese Empire.

It took Congress only thirty-three minutes to make up its mind. Isolationism was ended; Republicans voted with Democrats. In a united wave of fury against Japanese treachery, the American people turned with one accord from peace to war.

In Pearl Harbor the United States command had been utterly unprepared for the Japanese attack. When bombers appeared on the skyline the lookouts thought that they were Army planes on maneuvers. The first warning came when the bombs began to fall. With frantic haste the terse message went out: Air raid on Pearl Harbor.

As orders flashed, gun crews sprang into action, and men raced to their battle stations. On ships that were already blasted and burning the remaining guns blazed at the attackers; but they came on relentlessly, wave after wave.

The airfields at Hickham, Ford Island, Kanoehe and Ewa were aflame with spurting gasoline, and fragments of aircraft littered the runways. Crumpled hangars collapsed, burying men and planes in the debris. It was impossible to get fighters into the air to drive off the enemy.

The tragic and heroic story of that Sunday can never be fully told. Many of the men who could have told it died before it was over.

The bombers took a heavy toll in the harbor. The cruiser *Raleigh* suffered one of the first hits. A torpedo caught her amidships, and she listed with a gaping hole in her side. In Battleship Row, on the other side of Ford Island, dive bombers and torpedo bombers roared down the line. The warships were easy targets in the clear morning light. The *Oklahoma* was hit, and the *West Virginia* and the *Nevada*. The flagship *Arizona* was gravely damaged. Splintered steel piled high on the decks, smoke rose in blinding clouds and burning oil covered the surrounding water.

Eight minutes after the first bomb had fallen the *Oklahoma* foundered. With a shuddering roll the great ship turned over. Trapped below decks, sucked down and smothered in oil, many of her crew perished. Next in line lay the *West Virginia*. Battered from stem to stern, her guns silenced, she sank slowly into the harbor mud.

With a rending explosion the *Arizona* blew up. A Japanese torpedo had found its mark in the ammunition store. A great wall of flame enveloped the ship, and in that ghastly second more than a thousand men lost their lives.

The acts of gallantry on this day of disaster were countless. Men left their own ships when they were out of action and swam through burning oil to join their comrades at new battle stations. Officers continued to direct operations though they were mortally wounded, refusing to leave their posts for medical aid. As the world crashed around them the garrison of Pearl Harbor made history with its valor.

When the Japanese attack ended, Pearl Harbor lay under a pall of black smoke. The channels were jammed with sinking hulks; the airfields were a welter of smoldering planes; and thousands of men lay dead in the widespread wreckage. Of the fifteen men who won Congressional Medals of Honor in those few short hours, only four lived to receive their awards.

Total war had come to the American people.

2

The Way to War

WAR IN MODERN TIMES is a ghastly catastrophe. It spreads death and destruction and leaves a wake of sadness and suffering.

In the old days battles were fought by the armies and fleets of one nation against the armies and fleets of another. Now every man, woman, and child must share the danger. We are all in the front line, so we should certainly know what the fighting is about.

Who caused the Second World War, and why? What led up to it? How did the nations get themselves so mixed up?

The story starts at the end of the First World War in 1918. The Allies — the United States, Great Britain and the Commonwealth, France, Belgium, Serbia, Italy, and Japan — helped for three quarters of the time by Russia — defeated Germany, Austria, Hungary, Bulgaria, and Turkey. In four years of bitter fighting millions of men had died on the scarred and bloodstained battlefields of France, Belgium, northern Italy, Poland, Russia, the Balkans, and the Near East, and on the high seas.

The Allies were victorious but exhausted. And they were faced with another gigantic task: they had won the war, now they had to win the peace. Everyone was sick of slaughter, and it had become obvious that war brought ruin both to the victors and the vanquished.

Germany was the chief anxiety. Her armies had invaded France in 1871 and 1914, and her strength was a constant menace. The Allies hoped to reduce her to a state where she could not possibly attack again.

The leaders of the greatest powers conferred in an attempt to find a settlement that would keep the world at peace. After long discussions peace treaties were agreed upon by the warring nations, and the treaty which laid down Germany's future was signed in the gleaming Hall of Mirrors in the Palace of Versailles. The severe terms allowed Germany only enough troops and arms to police her own country; submarines and military aircraft were forbidden; and she was ordered to pay large reparations in goods and money to her conquerors. Germany was not permitted to keep any soldiers in the Rhineland, a province which borders on France, and German territory was pared off at the edges and given to her neighbors.

President Woodrow Wilson put before the great powers his plan for a League of Nations. To a war-weary world this seemed the perfect plan for lasting peace. Quarrels between nations were to be settled by an international court instead of by force, in the same way that personal quarrels are now settled in courts of law instead of being fought out in duels. There would be no need for arms.

The free countries of the world might well have prevented war had they stood together, but they lost sight of the danger and drifted apart. The first difficulty arose immediately after the First World War, when the United States refused to join the new League of Nations. President Wilson, heartbroken at the failure of his fine plan, fell ill and died soon afterward.

Warren G. Harding, who followed Wilson, told the American people that if they kept to themselves they would be able to stay out of European troubles. This is what many Americans wanted to hear, for they had helped to win one war and got little out of it. The chief result was that many nations now owed them money, and they were tired of Europe.

This was an understandable point of view. From the time when the early settlers braved the perils of the Atlantic in sailing ships, on through the centuries, America has been populated by men and women who decided to emigrate because they wanted to escape from old rules and rivalries. They risked everything to start afresh in a new land.

In the early days life had been hard and dangerous, but gradually the dreams of a promised land had come true. The American people had won freedom and riches, and they did not want to lose them.

They distrusted an organization like the League of Nations which might draw them back into the feuds of the Old World.

At that time the Americans felt very safe, well outside the range of a European war. The Atlantic had just been flown for the first time, and atomic power was unknown. The United States formed a policy of isolationism, which meant minding her own business and keeping out of other peoples' troubles.

The noble idea of the League of Nations failed because single nations, like single people, can be cruel or cowardly or lazy. After the First World War almost all the nations wanted peace, but they were drawn into a second war against their will. And each nation had its own problems that led up to the disaster.

After the peace treaty was signed, the German people were angry and resentful. They had not expected to be beaten, and it had come as a bewildering shock. The goose-stepping army which was their pride and joy had been disbanded; their majestic fleet was scuttled after its surrender; their emperor had fled; and Germany, now a republic, was no longer a great power. They were weighed down by the shame of defeat. Hard times followed. The German mark was devalued and money in the bank was worth practically nothing. People with savings lost all they had. Before the war the mark had been worth twenty-five cents; now it took thousands of marks to buy a loaf of bread and millions to buy an overcoat.

After a few years things began to improve, but in 1930 there was a world depression. Work in Germany was scarce. Men and women who were unemployed and starving grew desperate and rebellious. At this time the voice of an agitator called Adolf Hitler began to be heard, stirring up the people, using their poverty and distress for his own ends of revenge and self-glorification.

When Hitler's name first came into the news he had never made a success of anything. He was Austrian born, and as a young man lived in a home for tramps in the slums of Vienna, doing casual labor and very bad paintings. He had an interest in politics and a grudge against life.

He served as a corporal in the German Army during the First World War, but from 1918 onward directed all his energy to politics.

At first Hitler was ignored or despised by many Germans, but he won them over in two ways — by fascination and fear. The greatest mass orator of all time, he could sway vast crowds, whipping them into a frenzy of hysterical joy or fanatical hatred.

Hitler gave the German people new hope and new ambition. They were out of work, and he offered them jobs; they were cast down, and he revived dreams of power and glory. He was absolutely ruthless, a crook and a gangster, without conscience or pity. If the truth did not suit him he lied, and if people got in his way he had them murdered.

His followers called themselves National Socialists — Nazis for short — and chose as their symbol the crooked cross or swastika.

In 1933, at a time of acute political crisis and economic misery in Germany, Hitler took over the German Government by a mixture of trickery, violence, and high-powered oratory. He chose the new title of *Führer* (Leader) of the German people and always appeared in uniform. From that moment he ruled as a supreme dictator. People had been so lacking in any sense of leadership or national purpose that many of them blindly accepted the new system in which they did not have to think but merely to obey.

Hitler soon broke the peace treaty. Wheels began to turn in new armament factories, and uniformed guards paraded the streets. Then the barbed swastika cast its sinister shadow over Europe.

German girls and boys were enrolled in the Hitler Youth, an organization which seemed to them simply an exciting, patriotic game. They had no idea that they were being trained for war.

Hitler flattered the Germans, telling them that they were a master race, and he taught them to loathe and despise Jews, whom he blamed for all Germany's troubles. He tried to undo all Christian teaching. Never in the whole history of man have such savage massacres taken place as those of innocent Jews under the Nazis. And he preached *Le-*

bensraum (living space) for the German race,
knowing well that this claim could only be satisfied
by war.

Hitler also constantly warned the Germans that
communism was a world menace, and by that means
he won sympathy in countries where his methods
were otherwise condemned. He had set down all
these beliefs in a book called *Mein Kampf* ("My
Struggle"), but they were so fantastic that the rest
of the world did not take them seriously.

The Führer came to power six years before the
Second World War broke out, and in that time the
other nations watched the rise of nazism, first with
amazement and finally with terror. It had taken
them a long time to realize that the man they had
regarded as a ranting gutter politician could become so dangerous.

Italy was Germany's best friend in Europe, for
she had been governed since 1922 by another dictator, Benito Mussolini, a Fascist.

Fascism, like nazism, was a totalitarian system of
government: one man held all the power; there was
no political party in the country except his own; and
there were no free elections with honest voting. The
dictator's word was law. Mussolini was less blood-
thirsty than Hitler, but otherwise they saw eye to
eye.

Mussolini had started as a journalist, and, like
Hitler in Germany, he prospered at a time when
his country was sunk in a trough of financial dis-

tress and depression after the First World War. He called himself *Il Duce* (the Leader) of the Italian people. Mussolini's ruling passion was a lust for power. He pictured himself as another Caesar — head of a mighty empire, leader of modern legions, a war lord and statesman.

Although the Italian people did not share his ambitions and had never liked the Germans, they were led by Mussolini into a series of warlike acts in the years that led up to the Second World War. In 1935 he picked a quarrel with Abyssinia (now Ethiopia) in northeast Africa, a country of simple tribesmen, and made an easy conquest.

Italy already ruled Libya, Italian Somaliland, and Eritrea, and Mussolini claimed immense credit for the new addition to his North African Empire. Captured Abyssinian warriors were paraded through the flag-bedecked streets of Rome.

In 1936 Hitler and Mussolini together supported a rebel officer, General Francisco Franco, in an armed revolt against the Spanish Government. Civil war raged through Spain for nearly three years, and the dictators snatched at the chance of testing out their armaments, sending both men and machines.

The Spanish Government was backed by arms from Soviet Russia, and Communist volunteers of many nations fought with the government troops. The helpless Spanish people suffered poverty and peril while the three totalitarian states, Germany, Italy, and Russia, staged a dress rehearsal for total war.

General Franco was victorious and in 1939 became dictator of Spain. The Nazi and Fascist troops were called home to Germany and Italy.

In 1936 Hitler and Mussolini linked their countries together in what the Italian dictator described as the "Rome-Berlin Axis." The title was intended to tell the world that power in Europe revolved around a Nazi-Fascist hub. After this public demonstration of unity, both dictators proclaimed their devotion loudly and at great length.

In 1939 the two dictators became military and political allies when they signed what they called a "Pact of Steel." This alliance committed one partner to help the other should he be involved in a war.

Japan was another country preparing to endanger world peace. She wanted to build a great empire and was arming steadily. In 1940 she signed a pact with Germany and Italy, promising not to interfere in Europe if they would give her a free hand in the Far East. The Japanese hoped that if Hitler went to war he might defeat Great Britain and Holland, both of whom had interests in the Pacific.

The other nation blocking the way to Japanese expansion was the United States, whose powerful fleet was based at Pearl Harbor. Japan decided to continue preparations for a Pacific War while she waited to see how Hitler got on in Europe.

Russia had entered the First World War on the

side of the Allies. In March 1917, a revolution broke out and established a democratic government. On November 7, the Bolsheviks (Communists) led a second revolution and seized control of the government. Russia was now out of the war.

For a number of years before the Second World War, Russia, like Germany and Italy, was ruled by a dictator, Joseph Stalin, Secretary-General of the Communist Party of the Soviet Union. The country was still recovering from the ravages of revolution, and Stalin was desperately anxious to keep out of wars and to use all his money and man power to build up his own country.

France had been the chief victim of German aggression in the First World War. Almost all the battles in the west raged on French territory. In northern France the towns and villages were left in ruins and the countryside laid waste. Often peasants trying to get home when the fighting moved away from their district could not even find the village where they had lived.

Even more serious for France was the loss of young men. Each war memorial, from the tiny hamlets to the great cities, told its tragic tale, for nearly one fifth of all the fighting men of France were killed — a higher proportion than any other nation. Almost every French family lost someone.

It frequently happens that the finest and the bravest men are killed — those who would have made good leaders had they lived. The lack of young leadership had a tremendous effect on French policy between the wars. At the time when Hitler was rearming Germany and bold decisions were needed, France was governed by elderly men who were both weary and cautious. They believed that France would be well defended by the Maginot Line, a chain of massive forts which ran along most of her eastern frontier where Germany might attack. Because of this false sense of security French generals did not think it necessary to build up a fast-moving modern army.

When Hitler came to power he broke the terms of the Versailles peace treaty and marched an army into the Rhineland. France and Britain, who were chiefly concerned, looked on anxiously but did nothing to stop this march. So Hitler showed that he could gamble successfully on their desire for peace and get away with it. This was a milestone to war.

With other countries hanging back it became vital for Great Britain to take a strong lead in world affairs. But at the critical time when a mounting flood of tanks, guns, and aircraft was streaming out of German factories, Britain was governed by men who could not grasp the Hitler menace.

As the cries of "Heil Hitler!" multiplied in Germany and the thud-thud of marching storm troopers echoed through the land like a war drum, members of the British Government still clung to the hope of peace. Their goal was right, but their policy was mistaken.

In 1937, when Neville Chamberlain became Prime Minister, Britain was years behind Germany in arms and aircraft. But Parliament was not unduly worried, and Chamberlain found it impossible to believe that Hitler really meant war.

Winston Churchill was not a minister during these years. From his seat in the House of Commons he warned the government constantly and vividly of the increasing peril, but his words were little heeded.

In March 1938 Hitler took Austria. Tanks rolled over the mountain roads and down through the plains to Vienna; the *Luftwaffe* (German Air Force) roared across the skies. The conquest was over in a few days, while the world looked on helplessly.

Hitler's justification was that all German-speaking people belonged under one flag — his own.

That same year he threatened Czechoslovakia, an independent country that had been built up since 1918 around the ancient land of Bohemia, becoming in twenty years a united and prosperous nation. One part of Czechoslovakia — the Sudetenland — contained a number of German-speaking people who were now Czechoslovakian, and when Hitler demanded this area the Czech Government refused to give it up.

At this point Neville Chamberlain took upon himself the role of world peacemaker. He flew three times to see Hitler. On the last trip — September 29, 1938 — Chamberlain, French Premier Daladier, Hitler, and Mussolini signed the Munich Agreement, which dismembered Czechoslovakia.

The Czechs were not invited to participate in the negotiations. Instead, they were told by the British and French to surrender to Germany about one-third of their territory containing 3,600,000 of their people and three-fourths of their industrial resources. The Czechs had no choice but to give in. In return for this victory, Hitler gave Chamberlain his "solemn promise" to make no further claims on territory in Europe.

Chamberlain returned to London triumphant, waving the agreement and speaking with thankfulness of "peace in our time." He trusted Hitler, but what he had actually done was sell Czech independence in return for one year of uneasy peace.

Six months later Hitler ignored his own promise and, following his carefully laid plans, moved into the rest of Czechoslovakia. He knew that the British were not prepared to fight to rescue Czechoslovakia and to enforce the Munich Agreement; and he trusted that the French, who had a friendship pact with Czechoslovakia, would not fight alone. He was right; and so, without firing a single shot, he captured the whole Czech Army of one and a half million men and the Skoda works, one of the largest armament factories in Europe.

Then, at last, the world saw Hitler in his true colors, but by that time the peace-loving nations were so helplessly unready for war that there was little chance of checking his plans.

Poland was obviously marked down as the next Nazi victim. Great Britain and France announced that they would guarantee the Polish frontiers, promising to go to war if Germany attacked. They hoped to warn Hitler off — but it was far too late.

On August 22 came sinister news: Hitler had signed a pact of friendship with Stalin, dictator of Communist Russia, whom he had been denouncing fiercely for years as Germany's mortal enemy. This meant that the two dictators were buying each other off, in the hope of gaining time. It was a bitter blow to Britain and France, because they had hoped that Russia might side with them against Hitler. They could now see plainly that Hitler, having made his bargain with Stalin, would be free not only to destroy Poland but also to attack France, hoping to conquer her before Britain could come to her aid.

Later that same August the inevitable blow fell. The mighty Nazi forces struck at Poland, and by September 3 Britain and France had declared war on Germany.

So the way to war was laid when the peace-loving nations did not join forces against Hitler. They shut their eyes to the approaching danger. America stood aloof, while France lacked leadership after the First World War. Britain clung too long to false hopes of peace, and Hitler was convinced that nothing would provoke her to fight. His ambassador in London reported that "the British lion was stuffed." In this belief he was greatly mistaken.

Hitler was wrong too in his ideas about America.

He and his allies learned later, at bitter cost, that
Uncle Sam, though slow to anger, was a fierce and
mighty enemy.

3

The Invasion of Poland

ON THE THIRD of September, Neville Chamberlain, Prime Minister of Great Britain, broadcast to the world. He said that France and Britain were at war with Nazi Germany. His words, heavy with grief and solemnity, fell like stones on the hearts of the listening people.

In London after the broadcast there was a stunned silence. Then the hush was broken by the dreaded wailing of the air raid sirens — a dramatic and fearsome moment, for this seemed to be war in deadly earnest. Those who had air raid shelters went to them, and the rest just waited for the bombs to fall. In fact it was a false alarm, and the first bomb did not hit London for nearly a year.

Months of waiting followed the declaration of war. A horrible sense of doom hung over Britain and France. There was bitter fighting in far-off eastern Europe, but, except at sea, Britain and her ally had no part in it.

Men called it the "phony war." A.R.P. (Air Raid Precautions) became part of daily life. It was summer vacation, and while American children left the cities and went off to camp, British children were evacuated to the country for safety. It was a desolate sight — groups of boys and girls labeled with their destination collected at assembly points and were herded into overcrowded trains. They took with them only what they could carry, and they had no idea when they would see their parents again. Some of them cried, but most of them were dazed and obedient and very quiet. They were not frightened, because it was all so strange that they did not know what to be frightened of.

Gas masks were distributed, for it was thought the Germans would use poison gas, as they had in the First World War. People waited for hours in the crisp September sunshine, with an occasional upward glance at the clear skies; but the only visible objects were the silver barrage balloons, straining at their cables like plump watchdogs overhead.

Volunteers built walls of sandbags around the doorways of air raid shelters and important buildings, as a protection against bomb splinters. There was sand everywhere, and people scrunched it underfoot as they walked.

The blackout became law, and every window was darkened. The police and air raid wardens patrolled the streets, looking for cracks of light. The street lights were hooded and dimmed. At first it seemed impossible to get about at night, but soon people developed a sixth sense, like cats.

House-to-house collections were made for old iron, lead, and aluminum, to melt down for aircraft and guns. Families readily gave their porch railings, their saucepans, and their toy soldiers.

Meanwhile the world watched helplessly the massacre of Poland, as the full horror of Hitler's *Blitzkrieg* (lightning war) blazed over the country. In America, where many Poles lived, people read the place names with misery and fear for their families and friends.

Squadron after squadron of bombers took off from German airfields and crossed the Polish frontier with a thunderous roar. Waves of Stuka dive bombers screamed down to rooftop level in Polish cities, towns, and villages, dropped their bombs and raked the streets with machine-gun fire. There was no escape for the panic-stricken people.

Communications were wrecked, and the army was scattered by dive-bombing and demoralized by parachutists. There was little defense, as most of the Polish Air Force had been destroyed on its airfields before it ever left the ground.

A great cavalcade of tanks and armored cars poured into the country, and the Polish soldiers fought with desperate gallantry in isolated groups until they were mowed down.

The Russian dictator, Stalin, had made a bargain with Hitler a month earlier, and he marched in and grabbed a slice of eastern Poland. Britain and France could not get help to the Poles. Germany lay in the path, an impenetrable barrier. Sandwiched between Russia and Germany, Poland was doomed.

In four weeks the unequal struggle was over, and the Polish people entered into Nazi slavery.

Then, in November 1939, Stalin turned on Finland, making demands which the Finns could not possibly grant without surrendering their independence. This they refused to do, and the Red Army went into action; but a shock awaited the Russians, for where they had expected an easy victory, they had to fight a war.

The small Finnish Army defended its thousand-mile frontier with dogged courage. The land was deep in snow, and icy gales swept down from the north. The Finns were hardy, well trained, and used to the bitter weather. There were only a few brief hours of daylight, and Russian units found themselves constantly ambushed in strange country. Ski troopers swooped out of the snowy forests, made a lightning attack and disappeared like arrows into the Arctic night. After two months' fighting the Russian invaders had suffered heavy losses and gained no ground at all.

The free nations were filled with wonder and admiration at Finnish defiance, while the Germans watched the progress of their new Russian friends with scorn. Hitler decided that he could easily beat Russia when the time came.

The French and British governments wanted urgently to help Finland, but they were faced by the almost insuperable problems of fitting out an army to fight in the snow and then transporting it to a distant, northern battlefield. The only route lay through Norway, which was a neutral country.

By the time a decision had been made and a hundred thousand men assembled, Finland was beaten. The Russians had brought up huge reinforcements, and the Finns were overcome by sheer weight of numbers.

After his conquest of Poland, Hitler put forward a peace offer to Britain, lulling French fears of attack with soft words and false promises, hoping to split the Alliance. Hitler had never wanted to fight Britain and the Commonwealth, and he thought that after they had seen this exhibition of invincible might in Poland they would be glad to snap up a chance of peace.

Hitler misunderstood the British people and took their love of peace for cowardice. He forgot their proud traditions and that they "never have been slaves." The German dictator understood power, but he did not know about freedom. He suddenly discovered that there was no easy way out of the war. So he summoned his commanders to plan the conquest of Europe by armed force.

4

"The Navy's Here!"

For the Allies, the "phony war" dragged on all through that first winter of 1939–40. In Britain they waited for air raids that did not come. In France the small British Army stood alongside the French forces to meet the German attack. For eight long months — from the declaration of war in September until the following May — the two nations waited for Hitler to strike west.

But the British and French navies were in action, for there was no phony war at sea. Even before war was declared, seventeen Nazi U-boats (submarines) had been dispatched to war stations in the Atlantic. They had sneaked out and were lurking unseen, waiting to attack Allied shipping. Within a few hours of the declaration of war, the defenseless passenger ship *Athenia* was sunk in the Atlantic with the loss of one hundred and twelve lives.

When the war started Hitler had fifty-six U-boats,

and new ones were being launched every week. Admiral Doenitz commanded the U-boat fleet, and it was captained by men who had been trained for years and then carefully picked for their daring and skill. Of these underwater aces Lieutenant Prien proved one of the most efficient and dangerous.

In October 1939 the British Home Fleet was based at Scapa Flow, in Scotland. The anchorage was protected by islands, and the entrances sealed with booms, antisubmarine nets, and concrete blocks. The German spy system had reported one weakness in the defenses — a narrow channel between the mainland and a small island — and Prien was briefed to take his submarine into Scapa Flow and do as much damage as he could. It was a hazardous chance, but the prize was great.

At midnight on October 14, taking advantage of a high tide, he slipped through the narrow opening, grazing the defenses as he passed. It was a still, moonless night, and when he sighted the *Royal Oak* at the far end of the anchorage he fired a salvo of three torpedoes. He missed, but reloaded and fired again. His second salvo hit the battleship amidships, and in a few minutes she capsized and sank.

Prien escaped by the same channel, leaving no trace. It was not until the Nazis broadcast a triumphant report a few days later that the cause of the disaster was certain.

The pride of the German Fleet, the *Graf Spee*, under the command of Captain Langsdorff, had been secretly dispatched to the South Atlantic on

August 21, 1939, thirteen days before war was declared. She made her first kill on September 21st, and for three months she haunted the trade routes, sinking a succession of unarmed tankers and cargo ships.

Captain Langsdorff was a determined officer but not an ardent Nazi. He showed mercy to the crews of the merchant vessels, giving them time to take to the boats before sinking their ships. He picked them up and transferred them to his supply ship, the *Altmark*. Then he refueled the *Graf Spee,* disappeared into the wide reaches of the Atlantic and was not heard of again until his next victim sent out an SOS.

A British hunting group commanded by Commodore Harwood in the cruiser *Ajax* was sent to the area. It patrolled the South Atlantic from the African coast to South America, searching for the marauder, sweeping the ocean in narrowing circles, following the trail of destruction.

Commodore Harwood had always believed that a successful raider would, sooner or later, be tempted to take a rich and easy toll of the crowded shipping in the wide estuary of the River Plate in South America. Early in December distress calls showed that the *Graf Spee* was working northward. He decided that the time had come.

Though the *Graf Spee* was several thousand miles away from the River Plate, Commodore Harwood assembled the cruisers *Ajax, Achilles,* and *Exeter* at the mouth of the estuary and waited. It was a time of tense anxiety. For twenty-four hours the little force scanned the horizon. Then at early dawn on December 13 the lookouts sighted smoke. At last the long chase had ended.

The *Graf Spee* headed straight for the River Plate, and the cruisers separated and attacked from two sides. The range of their guns was shorter, and they made easy targets for the *Graf Spee*'s accurate fire; but they pressed in to attack. The battleship scored direct hits on the *Exeter*, but she fought on with damaged steering and only one gun firing until she listed too heavily to take aim.

The *Ajax* and *Achilles* attacked furiously, drawing the *Graf Spee*'s fire from the crippled *Exeter*. The *Ajax* was damaged and the British situation very serious, but the *Graf Spee* could not press home her advantage. Running short of ammunition and dogged by the battered cruisers, she made for the River Plate and took refuge in neutral waters at Montevideo.

The *Ajax* and *Achilles* patched up their battle scars as best they could and guarded the mouth of the river, while the aircraft carrier *Ark Royal* and the battleship *Renown* raced to their aid. But they could not arrive for five days, and the cruisers knew that it was a race against time; for although they had been joined by the cruiser *Cumberland*, they were still no match for the *Graf Spee*.

Two days before the reinforcements were due Captain Langsdorff left Montevideo and steamed down the river. The cruisers took up battle stations and braced themselves for the onslaught, but while they waited there was a deafening explosion. Without firing a shot the *Graf Spee* had been scuttled. Her captain believed that a strong force awaited him and, after cabling Hitler for instructions, he chose self-destruction rather than defeat.

The British ships speedily turned their attention from the *Graf Spee*, slowly settling into the estuary mud, to her supply ship, the *Altmark*. There was no sign of her near the River Plate, and they scoured the South Atlantic in vain.

The Admiralty was almost certain that three hundred British merchant seamen, handed over as prisoners from the *Graf Spee*, must still be on board.

The *Altmark* lay low for a while until the search slackened, then she made her way northward, hidden by the long dark, wintry nights. Passing around the north coast of Scotland wrapped in a blizzard, she soon gained the protection of neutral Norwegian waters and anchored in Jossing Fiord near Bergen.

Two months after the battle of the River Plate she was sighted by an aircraft of Coastal Command.

Captain Vian in the destroyer *Cossack* was sent to demand the release of British civilian prisoners, according to international law. The captain of the *Altmark* had managed to bluff the Norwegians, in whose waters the ship lay, so that they refused to allow a search, saying that she was an innocent merchant ship.

It was a tricky situation. The Germans had not yet overrun Norway, so she was still neutral. If

Captain Vian took the *Altmark* by force and found no prisoners he would be very much in the wrong. On the other hand, if he let the ship go and the seamen were there, they would be condemned to the horrors of a Nazi prison camp for the rest of the war.

Captain Vian told the Admiralty how matters stood and asked for orders. He got the signal: "Go ahead."

The *Cossack* entered the fiord in darkness and crunched her way through the pack ice, coming alongside the *Altmark* with grappling irons.

British sailors boarded the Nazi ship with dash and courage. They broke open the holds with a ringing shout: "The Navy's here!" Three hundred jubilant voices rose in reply.

The rescued men clambered on board the *Cossack*, and in twenty-four hours they were all safely back in England. The victory over the *Graf Spee* was complete.

In Britain, "The Navy's here!" became a slogan, something in which the people could have confidence during the dark days that lay ahead.

5

The Fall of Norway

Six months after his victory in Poland Hitler was ready to strike again. The attack on Norway was the lowest form of human conquest that the Nazis ever plotted. Even with the Austrians, Czechs, Poles, and Finns, some warning note was sounded, and the victims received a Nazi or Soviet ultimatum which put them on their guard. But the Norwegians were struck down by people who, talking eternal friendship, sneaked in with guns behind their backs.

Hitler coveted Norway for two reasons: first, to secure the whole supply of Swedish iron ore for his arms factories. Some of the world's finest ore, vital in time of war, is mined in the north of Sweden. It used to be shipped from Lulea in the Baltic, but each winter the port was icebound and traffic was held up.

So in 1902 the Swedish Iron Ore Company built a railroad over the mountains, across the Norwegian frontier to Narvik, a considerable engineering feat.

The line wound its way through nineteen tunnels in
the steep descent from the frontier pass to sea level.

The little fishing village on the bleak peninsula
was transformed into a busy and important port.
Narvik lies near the Arctic Circle, but because of
the Gulf Stream the harbor is almost free from ice.
In peacetime merchant vessels, flying the flags of all
nations, lined the long docks, waiting to ship the
precious cargo to world markets.

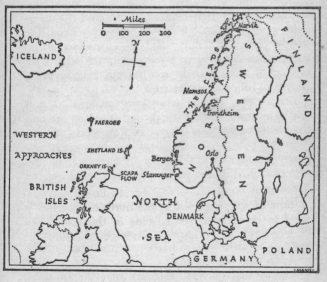

Norway and the northern approaches to Britain

Hitler's second reason for the attack on Norway was to gain protection for his shipping. The thousand-mile length of coast is pierced by long, narrow arms of the sea — the Norwegian fiords. Bounded by snow-capped mountains rising sheer from the water's edge, some of the fiords run inland for a hundred miles. They form deep, clear channels, navigable and sheltered, where German warships could anchor concealed from enemy eyes, ready to pounce on Allied shipping.

The waters off Norway are studded with hundreds of islands. Between the islands and the mainland runs a deep, protected seaway called the Leads. Here a warship could creep undetected on some secret mission, or a merchantman laden with ore could chug quietly south from Narvik for a thousand miles, unmolested.

Britain and France were very anxious to stop Germany from making use of both the iron ore and the sheltered waters. They badly needed bases in Norway, but they were unwilling to seize them, partly for fear of pushing her into the war on the side of Germany and partly because they respected her neutrality.

Hitler, however, had no such qualms. He wanted Norway, so he took her. First he made short work of Denmark, whose powers of resistance were nil and whose airfields and harbors formed part of the invasion plan for Norway.

It is typical of Nazi methods that the invasion forces included numbers of men who owed their lives to Norwegian generosity. The country had enjoyed peace for over a hundred years, and the people were simple and contented. Most of them were not rich, but hard-working and very hospitable. After the 1914 war there was famine in southern Germany and Austria, and when children were starving, Norwegian families took them into their homes and cared for them until they were well and strong.

The young Germans went to school with Norwegian children and learned the language and the kindly ways of the country. These were the men whom the Nazis sent back to Norway to destroy the people who had been so good to them.

At the beginning of 1940 Norway was still at peace, and the chief German diplomat in Oslo sent out invitations for a party and a film show to members of the Norwegian Government and many other influential people.

The film was *The Baptism of Fire*, a gruesome record of the war in Poland. The murderous violence and bloodshed from the beginning to the end of the campaign were flashed across the screen, and the terror and agony of the Polish people were shown in detail.

The audience was transfixed with horror. This was precisely what the Germans intended, for they wanted to make quite sure that the Norwegian leaders knew what happened to a country that opposed Hitler.

In the small hours of April 9, 1940, the German

Army overran Norway. The plans were carefully laid. In each of the four main ports — Oslo, Bergen, Trondheim, and Narvik — innocent-looking merchant ships lay alongside the wharves. But their holds were not so innocent; they were packed with invasion troops, fully armed, awaiting the signal to land.

The whole country had been riddled with German spies. Every public service, such as the police and the post offices, and every factory and shipping line contained enemy agents. A few Norwegians had also been recruited to the Nazi cause and had received their orders.

Rumors of a German invasion had reached the government the day before, but the bulk of the people were utterly unprepared, and when they woke up on the morning of April 9 the Nazis had already taken over a large part of the country.

The Norwegian people were dazed, for they had trusted the Germans. It seemed impossible that these troops who arrived with bands playing, many of them speaking fluent Norwegian, had come to enslave them. The bands were just a bluff. One of them arranged itself in the main square in Oslo and played sentimental German songs, American hit tunes, and "Roll out the Barrel." There was no shooting at this point.

The most important Norwegian agent of the Nazis, Major Quisling, proclaimed himself Prime Minister and broadcast traitorous commands, forbidding resistance. The word "quisling" found its way into wartime vocabulary as a term of contempt for men who worked for the Nazis against their own country.

As the full horror of the betrayal dawned, resistance sprang up. King Haakon and his government left Oslo, set up headquarters a hundred miles away and tried to organize a defense.

Norway had no standing army; her young men all did a term of military training and then went back to civilian life. In the general confusion it was impossible to mobilize them, for they were scattered and had no uniforms, weapons, or commanders. Little bands formed up under any officer who happened to be on the spot. They had no tanks to meet the German armor and only about a dozen aircraft against hundreds, but the Norwegians were not short of courage. Shooting is a national sport in Norway, and they made good use of any ammunition they could lay their hands on. The stanch Viking spirit dies hard.

The Nazis learned several bitter lessons in the early days. They commandeered Oslo bus drivers to carry troops, each bus carrying sixty men. The first three drivers took their buses over a precipice, crashing into a deep ravine below to certain death. The Germans just succeeded in stopping the fourth bus, and after that they left the bus drivers respectfully alone.

Soon little knots of Norwegians took up positions in the path of the advancing Germans and clung to them fiercely, fighting day and night.

Even in peacetime it is not easy to travel in Norway. The mountains are so high and the valleys so steep that roads and railroads have to be cut and tunneled at great expense. The small population can seldom afford the high cost, so the fiords are often the main roads of Norway. Little steamers ply from one village to another, delivering letters and food, collecting fish for the towns, linking up communities which are days apart by a land route. In wartime little news filtered from one fiord to the next, and the fighting was scattered and lonely. Men did not know how their comrades were doing.

The British and French War Cabinets were in a grievous dilemma, without an instant to lose. The danger of having the German Fleet in complete control of the Norwegian seaboard was clear. Apart from this they wanted urgently to save the Norwegian people from Nazi aggression. They were faced with the twin problems of getting enough troops together when they could not be spared from the defense lines in France, and then of landing them in Norway where the Germans already held the airfields and harbors.

Yet, nine days after the Nazi invasion, Allied troops landed near Trondheim in southern Norway and joined up with scattered Norwegian units who were fighting heroically.

It was a losing battle from the first moment. The Allied forces never had a landing stage big enough to put ashore tanks or heavy armor, and the Germans held command of the air.

Nazi bombers took off from the Stavanger airfield and bombed the Norwegian and Allied units out of existence if they showed a head aboveground in daylight. They had to hide in the forests until dusk.

The weather, too, was on Hitler's side, for the whole country was snowbound; and although the Allied troops had warm clothing, they were weighed down by heavy kits. Sometimes, sinking deep at every step, it took them three or four hours to cover a mile; it was a test of endurance to move at all, let alone fight.

British bombers from their home bases tried to support the army. They flew four hundred miles across the North Sea to find their targets; but fuel was short, and when they had dropped their bombs they were faced by the long flight home. The Fleet Air Arm attacked gamely with Skuas, but they were always outnumbered. The British and French fleets tackled the enemy wherever and whenever they could find them.

On April 27 after ten days of hopeless fighting, the situation became desperate, and a retreat was ordered. Most of the Allied troops got out, evacuated by their navies, but there were losses and hairbreadth escapes.

As the Allied forces withdrew, the Norwegian troops moved northward, determined to hold the Narvik area. The Allied Chiefs of Staff had been anxiously watching Narvik, and just before the German invasion the Navy had laid mines in the Leads, south of the port, to block passage of the iron ore.

On April 9 news came through that Narvik had fallen — betrayed by a Norwegian Nazi commander and captured by the troops smuggled there in merchant ships. A strong German naval force was seen heading north to reinforce the German garrison in the town.

A flotilla of British destroyers, supported by the battleship *Warspite*, set out in pursuit. At early dawn they steamed into Narvik Fiord, made their perilous way through the narrow, rocky passage, and took the enemy by surprise. In a series of battles, with the loss of two destroyers, they hunted down and wiped out the entire enemy force.

In the following month, Hitler's armies overran Belgium, Holland, and Luxemburg. On June 5, German military might converged on France. As a result, the British and French governments were compelled to withdraw the last remnants of their forces from Norway, and on June 9 the fighting in Norway ended, King Haakon, the Norwegian government, and many men of the Army, Navy, Air Force, and Merchant Marine escaped to Great Britain, where they carried on the fight for freedom.

The gains lay heavily on the German side of the scales. They had won naval and air bases flanking the British Isles, and they built submarine pens at Trondheim, only two hundred miles from the Shetlands, and kept them stocked for the rest of the war. Swedish iron ore flowed into Germany, and Hitler, who appeared to be invincible, had added another name to his victory list.

The Allies could mark up two things in their favor: a number of German ships at the bottom of the sea or putting in for repairs; and the drain on Nazi man power from policing Norway.

The Nazi occupation forces never did enjoy their stay there, for they were hated and despised. They met with sinister accidents on dark nights, and savage reprisals entirely failed to expose the Norwegian culprits.

A story is told of a plane crashing into the sea off the Norwegian coast. Some fishermen set out in their boat to look for survivors, but they returned empty-handed.

"It was a German plane," they said.

"But were none of them alive?" asked one of the spectators.

"Well, one of them said he was, but you know what liars these Germans are," was the fisherman's reply.

The defeat in Norway had a profound effect on the British people. They were shocked and ashamed, and indignation swept the country. Neville Chamberlain fell before the storm. He resigned the premiership and was succeeded by the vigorous leadership of Winston Churchill, at the head of a National Coalition Government.

6

The Battle of France

THE CHANGE of leadership in Britain and the opening of Hitler's offensive on the Western Front made May 10, 1940, a momentous day. The two events, each of the highest importance, took place within a few hours.

When Winston Churchill accepted the invitation of King George VI to form a National Coalition Government, it was a matter of wartime urgency, for the phony war was over and the Allies faced a mighty avalanche of steel and fire.

In peacetime, democratic countries like the United States and Britain consider the party system the best way of running their governments. The leaders have to face criticism and uphold their decisions in open debate. Therefore the brains and energy of the country are used partly in authority and partly in opposition, either as a spur or a brake. But in 1940 Britain felt that no talent should be wasted. All the wisdom, strength, and courage of the nation was harnessed to the same team, and people discarded their party slogans.

Winston Churchill assumed the offices of Prime Minister and Minister of Defense, and called to his aid the best men he could find to do the jobs. Only their patriotism and brains counted — not their party.

On May 13 the Prime Minister told the House of Commons about the new government and asked for a vote of confidence. The House heard on that solemn occasion one of the most stirring speeches ever delivered to a gathering in a time of crisis. Winston Churchill said:

I have nothing to offer but blood, toil, tears and sweat.

We have before us an ordeal of the most grievous kind. We have before us many, many long months of suffering and struggle. You ask, what is our policy? I will say: It is to wage war by sea, land and air, with all our might and with all the strength that God can give us; to wage war against a monstrous tyranny, never surpassed in the lamentable catalogue of human crime.

That is our policy: You ask, what is our aim? I can answer in one word: Victory — victory at all costs, victory in spite of all terror, victory however hard and long the road may be; for without victory there is no survival.

The British people had found a leader. Now they knew where they were going.

The time had come for Britain to shoulder the heavy burdens of battle. The Allied Chiefs of Staff had known since the declaration of war in September 1939 that sooner or later the Germans would attack in western Europe. It was agreed that as the French and British armies were not strong enough to take the offensive, the best they could do was to assemble all their available forces and make ready to meet the onslaught when it came.

In the early days of rearmament after Munich, Britain concentrated mainly on her Navy and Air Force. Her Army was well trained, but small. In May 1940 she had only nine divisions in France, compared with the hundred and five divisions of the French. It was clear that with France's great military tradition and her lion's share of the military contribution, the Supreme Commander of the Allied Armies must be French.

So General Gamelin, a distinguished soldier, veteran of the First World War, was placed in supreme command.

In the field was General Billotte, commanding the First Group of Armies, including the British Expeditionary Force of nine divisions. This group of armies stretched from the northern end of the Maginot Line at Longwy up to the coast near Dunkirk.

The British Expeditionary Force (B.E.F.) was commanded by General Lord Gort, serving under the French Supreme Commander. He faced his new responsibilities with a fine fighting record behind him from the First World War.

The aged Marshal Pétain, hero of the Battle of Verdun twenty-five years earlier, was a very influential figure in France at this time, and people did not realize that at the age of eighty-four he had many out-of-date ideas.

In the German military sphere, the Supreme Command of all the Armed forces was exercised by Hitler, who made the decisions, took the credit, and was intensely jealous of any rival success or publicity.

The Commander in Chief of the German armies, Colonel General von Brauchitsch, owed his job to Hitler. An ardent Nazi, he had helped to rebuild the German Army, but he was torn at times between loyalty to his master and distrust of his military tactics.

Colonel General von Rundstedt commanded Army Group A, which contained the whole German *Panzer* (armored) force of ten divisions. He was one of the ablest soldiers in the German Army, proving ruthlessly successful in Poland, and he supported Hitler against von Brauchitsch in planning the main attack through the Ardennes country, instead of following the old route through Belgium.

Colonel General Bock, a less outstanding figure, commanded Army Group B.

The whole German force on the Western Front comprised a hundred and twenty-six divisions, including the ten Panzer divisions, with nearly three thousand armored vehicles and at least a thousand heavy tanks.

Against this force the Allies had assembled a hundred and three divisions, including nine British. It

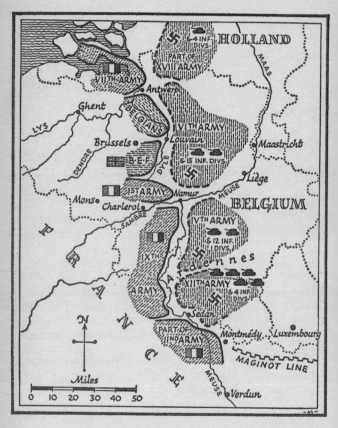

The battlefield before the German breakthrough,
May 1940

was hoped that twenty-two Belgian divisions and ten Dutch would fight with them when the moment came. The French had six armored divisions, but because they did not know where the main attack would fall they were dispersed over a wide area.

You will see from the map how these forces were disposed.

The Allied Air Forces were outnumbered about three to one by the Luftwaffe, and they also lacked speed and armament. They made up in flying skill and sheer courage for some of the technical failings, but it was a terribly costly business. The British Battle, Blenheim, and Lysander bombers and the Hurricane fighters were based behind the front, where fifty-nine new airfields were in the making.

Battles are won by strategy as well as strength. In France, largely owing to the advanced age of many of her generals, the General Staff judged warfare by the conditions of 1914. They had not grasped the mobility and power of modern armament, but pinned their faith and hope on permanent forts and natural obstacles. Their strategy was hopelessly old-fashioned.

The southern part of the French frontier was protected by the Maginot Line. It was manned by nine divisions and believed to be impregnable.

The central section of the frontier was in the region of the Ardennes — wooded, hilly country that was considered unsuitable for armored warfare. Marshal Pétain had said, "This sector is not dangerous," and it was therefore guarded only by second-class troops, with very few regular officers, and lightly screened by horse-drawn artillery. This was the crucial error that wrecked the whole Allied defense scheme.

The northern part of the front, along the Franco-Belgian frontier, was the area where the Germans were expected to strike, so the British Expeditionary Force was placed here, flanked by the French First and Seventh Armies. The Allies were so sure that the enemy would attack in the north that they made no arrangements to meet a main attack elsewhere.

It was always realized that Holland could not be protected from Nazi invasion, but as the Dutch had been bypassed by one war they hoped they might be lucky again.

The case of Belgium was quite different. The Allies repeatedly tried to make plans with the Belgian Government, but the Belgians refused to budge one inch from their neutrality. All the French and British could do was to build up their strength on the French side of the frontier and hope for the best.

The Allies had worked out two plans of action to deal with the expected enemy attack in the north.

1. Plan E.   To move forward one day's march to the river Escaut (Schelde), take up positions and prepare for the German onslaught.

2. Plan D.   To move farther forward a distance of sixty miles to the river Dyle.

They were both moderately good defensive positions, and Plan D had the advantage of saving more of Belgium and of probably joining up with the Belgian Army. The final choice was to be made by the Supreme Commander when the time came.

So at the beginning of May, while reports of massed German troop movements filtered through, the Allied armies waited. They were years behind in preparation, but they had done what they could in the eight months' respite since war was declared.

Meanwhile, the Nazis had gained battle experience and confidence in Poland and Norway. Germany resounded with the clang of massive arms pouring out along the assembly lines and Hitler's voice screaming at the people in a frenzy of fury and hatred against Britain.

At early dawn on May 10 the storm broke over Holland. Armored divisions rushed the frontier bridges, and parachutists landed behind the Dutch lines.

The Dutch believed that they had an impassable water-line defense. At a given signal the sluices in the frontier dikes were to be opened, and a huge body of water would flow out in front of the invading army. In fact, like everyone else, they underestimated the speed and cunning of the Nazi assault, and most of the sluice-opening machinery was captured before the Dutch frontier guards had time to operate it.

The Dutch Army fought hard and lost a great many men. The Luftwaffe attacked airfields and harbors. Then they laid waste the center of Rotterdam with systematic savagery. After five days the

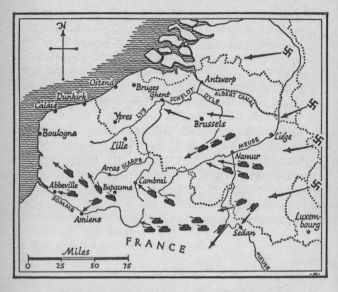

Nazi Panzer divisions after the breakthrough

Dutch royal family was brought to England by the
Navy. Holland was beaten.

In France the Supreme Command decided on
Plan D, and British Headquarters received the
order: "Plan D today. Zero hour 1300. 12 Lancers
may cross before zero. Wireless silence canceled
after crossing frontier. Air reconnaissance com-
mence forthwith."

The B.E.F. and the French First and Seventh

Armies advanced sixty miles through Belgium to the banks of the river Dyle. They joined up with the Belgian Army, which had been driven back by the first impact, and took up their positions without serious hindrance. Unfortunately, the Belgians had failed to blow up some of the bridges in the path of the German advance — a grave handicap to the Allied armies.

The mighty frontier fortress of Eben Emael was captured by German storm troopers almost before the Belgian defenders knew they were at war. The fort had been built by German engineers who handed the plans to the Nazi High Command.

Already, on the night of May 12, bad news started to come from the Ardennes region, and it became clear that the Allied system of defense was wrong. General Bock, attacking Belgium, had only twenty divisions with three Panzer divisions. General von Leeb, facing the Maginot Line, had seventeen divisions and no Panzers. But General Rundstedt, thrusting into the Ardennes, had forty-four divisions and seven Panzers. This was the main attack.

The German armor was not impeded at all by the rugged Ardennes country. The tanks ground their way up the hills with relentless certainty, and the French cavalry fled before the wall of steel. The Germans reached the river Meuse about ten miles inside France, near Sedan, on the night of May 12, after only two days fighting.

Then the Nazi dive-bombing started. The raw troops who were defending the riverbank were paralyzed. They had neither the arms nor the experience to stand up to the murderous fire. They collapsed, and on May 14 the Germans crossed the Meuse on a front of twelve miles.

The Allied front was breached; it was a major disaster.

From the very beginning of the battle the Allied Air Forces were sent into action. The Hurricanes took heavy toll of the German bombers; but the Blenheims and Battles were designed to bomb targets in enemy territory with fighter cover. Dive-bombing in support of an army was a new feature in war. The German Stukas were built for the job, but the British bombers were not.

Nevertheless, they took off constantly. They flew low to attack troop concentrations, bridges, and communications, sustaining fearful losses, flying sortie after sortie because their numbers were small and the need so great. In one afternoon in the Ardennes sector, out of seventy R.A.F. aircraft forty were lost. The tattered squadrons were re-formed, and fought on.

The news from the Ardennes grew worse and worse. The German armies were pouring through a widening gap, and although French resistance was fierce in places, orders from the top were confused and halfhearted, and most of them were out of date by the time they reached the front.

The French Supreme Command never recovered from the shock of their mistaken policy. Depression and defeatism had crept into high places.

On May 18, as a last resort, the French government was re-formed. Premier Reynaud also acted as Minister of Defense. He made Georges Mandel, a man of dogged courage and unflinching determination, Minister of the Interior. Marshal Pétain became Deputy Premier, and the Supreme Commander, General Gamelin, was replaced by General Weygand, who was seventy-four years old.

On May 20 the German Panzers reached the French coast at Abbeville, and the Allied armies were cut in half. This was the beginning of the end of the Battle of France.

On the same day the "Weygand Plan" was produced. General Weygand proposed that dual Allied attacks from north and south could first isolate and then destroy the German divisions that had reached the sea. General Billotte reported that the French First Army was exhausted and could be driven no farther. The B.E.F., having been less hard pressed, was the only stanch fighting force left in the north.

Driving away from the conference, General Billotte was severely injured in a car crash. He died two days later — a great tragedy, for he was the only man who held the last shreds of control over the French armies. Individual commanders fought stubbornly, but the last hope of spirited leadership was gone.

The B.E.F. had been fighting well on the northern section of the front. General Gort had been keenly aware since the first days of the German breakthrough that unless the gap was plugged his troops would be left in a dangerous position. Their vital lines of supply, stretching undefended across France in the path of the advancing enemy, would be severed — and the British Army trapped. They would have no ammunition, no food, and no retreat but the sea.

It was decided that the B.E.F., with the Belgian Army on its left and the French First Army on its right, should withdraw to the river Escaut. The British troops were mystified. They had advanced and then held onto their positions in the face of active German pressure, and they felt they were not doing too badly; yet now they were ordered to retire.

Retreat was difficult, because all the roads leading west were jammed with refugee traffic. Rich and poor alike were fleeing before the German armies — families riding in expensive cars and packed into farm wagons; peasants driving cattle before them; men and women with children on their backs and their worldly possessions piled high on wheelbarrows. Most of them had no idea where they were going, but they came on in a stream of human misery. Many of them had made the same heartbreaking journey in 1914.

Communications from French Headquarters grew increasingly irregular and contradictory, and it became clear that General Gort would have to take full responsibility for the conduct of the B.E.F. The Panzer divisions were racing for the Channel ports. The area held by the Allied troops in northern

France was shrinking hourly, and the Belgian Army was hard pressed and cracking. The only hope of saving the B.E.F. was to form a bridgehead around Dunkirk and trust to the Navy to get them out. So the fighting withdrawal to the sea began. Ostend was lost, Boulogne fell on May 23, and Calais was being held for a limited time at supreme cost.

Each hour that Calais stood gave thousands of men a chance for safety. It was decided that the small British garrison in that town should fight, with no respite and no hope of deliverance, to the bitter end.

For three days the defenders held up the advance of the German Army. They manned the bastions which surrounded the old town, and only when the walls crumbled under the dive-bombing and shell-fire did they fight their way back through the battered streets to the Citadel.

At last, on the afternoon of May 26, the enemy broke in and captured the remnants of the gallant force. Many of the men were wounded; they entered into long years of captivity, but they had completed their task gloriously.

On May 27 catastrophe overtook the Belgian Army. The Germans broke through their lines, and King Leopold asked for an armistice.

7

The Miracle of Dunkirk

THE BRITISH EXPEDITIONARY FORCE and the French
First Army plugged the gaping hole left in their
line by the Belgian surrender. They built up a
beachhead around Dunkirk, a defended area stretching twenty miles along the coast and five miles inland. The B.E.F. had been constantly on the move
for a week, retreating all the time. There was no
panic and no disorder, for although the men were
exhausted they never lost their fighting spirit. They
were well led; Generals Alexander, Brooke, and
Montgomery were among the commanders.

The B.E.F. defended the beaches, and the French
First Army the section around Dunkirk town.

On May 28 the evacuation began — "Operation
Dynamo." It went on for nine days.

The Navy had known for a week that the crisis
was approaching, and Admiral Ramsey, in command
at Dover, across the Channel on the English coast,

had collected every available naval ship. Destroyers, sloops, corvettes, mine sweepers, and motor torpedo boats were assembled, awaiting orders. But the prospects were gloomy, for with the tremendous pressure of the German advance it seemed an impossible task to get the men away in time.

No one could have foreseen the strange and magnificent sequel. The seafaring population of England rose to the emergency in a great surge of defiant anger, bringing to the rescue every vessel that could float. The queerest armada in history was gathered together, ships of every size and shape, sharing a single stubborn purpose.

Passenger ferry steamers from all the Channel ports, barges from the Thames estuary, tramp steamers and lifeboats from all along the coast, Southend pleasure boats, oyster dredgers from Burnham-on-Crouch, motorboats dug out from little shipyards and the quiet reaches of the Thames, all the tugs from the Port of London, fishing boats from every south coast village, weekend yachts with converted motorcar engines, speedboats and rowboats — all were there. The Thames fireboat *Massey Shaw*, armed only with her fire pumps, made two trips and brought off over a hundred men. The old destroyer *Sabre* set a record with ten trips. Belgian, French, Dutch, and Polish vessels joined the assorted fleet. The names tell a story in themselves — the *Canterbury, Medway Queen, Brighton Belle, Maid of Orleans, Vrouw van Vlaanderen, Frightened Lady, Ma*

*Joie, Ave Maria, Mona's Isle, Lazy Days, Gay Cru-
sader, Auntie Gus, Bonny Heather,* and *Our Lizzie*
— with hundreds of others.

Everyone sailed under naval orders; but each man
had to use his own wits as well, for the situation
changed from day to day and hour to hour. The
only thing that never changed was the danger; it
was there all the time, on every side and overhead.
The Germans battered the sea and the beaches mercilessly, shelling from the land and bombing from
the air. There were many casualties in ships and
men, and the sea was littered with wrecks, waterlogged craft, and floating bodies. British-based Hurricanes and Spitfires and planes of the Fleet Air
Arm beat off the Luftwaffe, but they came back
again and again.

The defense at the outer ring of the perimeter
held firm. Unit after unit engaged the enemy while
their comrades escaped. Then they moved back into
the beachhead, and the area shrank as more men
embarked. The troops took shelter in the dunes,
crouching in the warm sand, waiting to be called.
At night the whole scene was illuminated by the
flames from the oil tanks set alight in Dunkirk, and
by day the billowing black smoke hung like a
shroud.

As their turn came the men formed long lines
curling over the flat, yellow beaches into the sea. A
naval officer told how he brought his boat alongside
what he thought was a breakwater. It turned out to
be a human pier of men standing up to their waists

in water, quietly waiting to be picked up. They had infinite faith in the Navy.

Some of the men trudged to the harbor and boarded ships at the jetty, some were killed on the beaches within sight of freedom. The wounded were carried aboard by their friends. They lost their equipment and often their clothes — everything except their courage. After the first three days the order was given to evacuate the French equally with the British.

The rescue craft steamed out of the English harbors in the late afternoon, to arrive off the beachhead at night. A tramp steamer or tug would take in tow a long string of smaller boats to ferry the men from the shallow waters to the larger ships waiting offshore. Destroyers nosed through the fleet like terriers, fighting off dive bombers, picking up men from sinking ships, controlling the seething mass of shipping. The Merchant Marine unhesitatingly took their ships into the barricade of fire, and men worked on and on without sleep until they collapsed.

Volunteers from every walk of life manned the little ships: amateur sailors from offices and banks, from shops and factories; boys on leave, hotelkeepers, and cooks. Many of them could not read a compass, but they headed for the glare which flooded the sky over Dunkirk.

On June 4 "Operation Dynamo" ended.

The job was done. Altogether 338,226 men of the

Allied forces were saved from what had seemed certain death or captivity. Complete disaster had been averted, and the bulk of the British Expeditionary Force lived to fight again.

Many of the gallant little ships were missing, but the rest came home, proudly bearing battle scars. The Spitfire trails faded from the Dunkirk skies, and silence settled over the beaches.

On June 4, in the House of Commons, Winston Churchill warned the nation that wars were not won by evacuations. He went on to tell the world:

We shall go on to the end. We shall fight in France, we shall fight on the seas and oceans, we shall fight with growing confidence and growing strength in the air, we shall defend our island whatever the cost may be, we shall fight on the beaches, we shall fight on the landing-grounds, we shall fight in the fields, and in the streets, we shall fight in the hills; we shall never surrender.

The position in France grew steadily worse. On June 10 Mussolini declared war on France and Britain, and attacked on the French Mediterranean frontier — a stab in the back to snatch a share of the spoils of victory.

The French Army could no longer even be organized into an orderly retreat; and on June 12 Paris was declared an open city, the government retiring to Tours.

At this point Britain offered France national union: the two countries would fight on as a single nation, sharing all the resources of Britain and the Commonwealth in the cause of freedom. The French turned the offer down.

There was a violent difference of opinion in the highest ranks of the French Government. Some stanch patriots like General de Gaulle were determined to carry on the fight from North Africa. But the defeatists were too numerous, and Marshal Pétain, aided by General Weygand, Admiral Darlan, and Pierre Laval, sued for an armistice on June 16.

Hitler staged a dramatic setting for his revenge. The Nazi terms were dictated to the French in the same railroad car, brought from its Paris museum and placed in the identical spot in the Forest of Compiègne, where the Allied terms had been handed out to the Germans on November 11, 1918.

The Nazi terms were harsh.

The French people and territory were to be put to work for the Germans and used against Britain.

The Germans would occupy the northern half of France and all the ports. Wireless transmission was forbidden, so the French were cut off from communication with the free world.

All French prisoners taken by the Germans were to stay in captivity until the end of the war, but all German prisoners were to be released instantly. These included four hundred airmen, mostly shot down by the R.A.F. M. Reynaud had made a prom-

ise to hand them over to the British, but he had
lost the power to keep it; Winston Churchill said,
"We shall have to shoot them down again."

All the French forces were to be demobilized and
disarmed, including the fleet.

A tragic event followed — one which might have
left lasting resentment between the French and
British people. The British Government knew that
the French would never willingly use their fleet
against their former allies, for they had given their
solemn word. But the Germans had taken over
France lock, stock, and barrel; their word was law,
and they had fearsome means of enforcing it. The
Germans had said they would not use the French
fleet, but a Nazi promise had proved to be worth-
less. The British dared not risk the menace of the
splendid French fleet in Nazi hands.

In July, just after the French armistice, urgent
messages were sent to French admirals in the Mediterranean, begging them to bring their ships to Britain or to scuttle them.

The pleas were refused, because Admiral Darlan,
Commander in Chief of the French Fleet, had come
to terms with the Nazis. So, on July 2, 1940, the
British Mediterranean fleet attacked. So many ships
were sunk or damaged that the French Navy ceased
to be a powerful weapon on either side. The action
was a dreadful one, dictated by dire necessity.

Marshal Pétain headed a new government in
France — the Vichy Government — served by Dar-

lan, Laval, and a group of defeatist politicians. General de Gaulle escaped to England where he started the Free French Resistance Movement, which grew into a powerful force for freedom.

8

The Battle of Britain

WHEN THE BATTLE of France was over, Britain and the Commonwealth stood alone.

Winston Churchill broadcast a warning to the nation:

The whole fury and might of the enemy must very soon be turned on us. Hitler knows that he will have to break us on this island or lose the war. . . . Let us brace ourselves therefore to our duties, and so bear ourselves that, if the British Empire and its Commonwealth last for a thousand years, men will say "This was their finest hour."

At the end of June Hitler entered Paris in triumph. He drove down the Champs Élysées in uniform, his Iron Cross on his chest. He visited Napoleon's tomb and went up the Eiffel Tower to survey the beautiful city he had conquered. So far he had kept his promise to the German people; the French nation was humbled, and the German shame of 1918 partly avenged.

Hitler made another peace offer to Britain, always hoping to end the war the easy way. As she steadfastly refused to give in, the Führer mobilized his forces for her complete destruction. He was pressed for time, as the German people had not been led to expect a long war; and it was vital to launch the invasion fleet across the Channel before the autumn gales set in.

Nothing could be done while the R.A.F. was still active. The Nazi generals had seen enough of the Hurricanes and Spitfires over Dunkirk to realize that it would be suicidal for their armies to set sail without command of the air.

Field Marshal Göring, head of the Luftwaffe, was elated by his victories in Poland, Norway, Holland, Belgium, and France, and boasted to Hitler that it would take only a few weeks to smash the R.A.F. He regrouped his "invincible" forces and established them on the newly won airfields, while crack parachute divisions were brought west ready for the drop on Britain.

At the same time strings of landing barges slipped along the coast by night and assembled in the French and Belgian harbors. Concentrations of troops, armor, and supplies mounted steadily, waiting to embark as soon as the R.A.F. was defeated.

In Britain the whole population was fiercely resolved to defeat the enemy. Every man, woman, and child was a part of the island garrison. The miracle of Dunkirk had been accomplished. Their hearts were filled with courage, and there was no thought of surrender.

Defenses bristled everywhere; the beaches were mined, tank traps and concrete pillboxes appeared along the roads, and barbed wire sprawled across the countryside.

Invasion might come by sea or air or both together, and everyone recalled the part played by German parachutists in the conquest of Poland and Holland. So throughout Britain people prepared to meet an airborne landing. Nothing was left to help a wandering parachutist to find his way. Railroad station nameboards were removed from all platforms, and every road signpost was taken down. Vehicles were immobilized each night by the removal of a vital part. In case of parachute or seaborne invasion, church bells would be rung as a public warning.

An appeal went out for volunteers to enroll in a Home Guard to fight in their home towns and villages if the Germans came. Soon the ranks rose to a million. Weapons were very scarce, and at first the men drilled with shotguns and old revolvers. Later, when supplies improved, they were given weapons and uniforms.

Factories worked around the clock to refit the Army, but there was a dismal shortage of every kind of gun and ammunition. None could be spared for training or practice — every round had to be hoarded to use against the enemy.

In response to urgent demands, America set out to produce the arms that Britain needed. It was clear that without swift aid Britain might perish and the last outpost of freedom in Europe be lost.

Air Chief Marshal Sir Hugh Dowding was in charge of Fighter Command of the R.A.F. These were the squadrons who, outnumbered but undaunted, fought the Battle of Britain. Their pilots were the famous "few," only about a thousand all told. Before the war many of them had been amateur pilots who flew for fun; now they flew in deadly combat. With firm comradeship, enduring heroism, and unfailing high spirits these men carried the fate of Britain in their hands.

The R.A.F. squadrons had been enriched by eager volunteers from other countries. In America men threw up their jobs, crossed the Atlantic and joined the "few." Their country was not yet at war, but they came of their own accord to fight for freedom. Later they formed the Eagle Squadrons of the R.A.F. and proudly wore a spread eagle on their uniform. Canadians, as well as Czechs and Poles who had escaped from Nazi Europe, added their squadrons to the R.A.F. In all, twenty-five fighter squadrons assembled on seven airfields in southeast England and waited.

Early in July the Luftwaffe started attacking the Channel convoys. The fighter squadrons went up after them, and dogfights broke out high over the narrow seas as the Hurricanes and Spitfires dived on the bomber formations. People on the white cliffs watched as Dorniers and Junkers plunged down in flaming corkscrews.

These were testing raids. The Luftwaffe soon changed its tactics. On July 10 hundreds of German bombers, heavily escorted by Messerschmitts and Heinkels, systematically attacked airfields and radar posts in southern England.

This was the critical phase, when Göring planned to blast the R.A.F. from the skies and runways and open the road to London. Day after day the raids followed, with ever-increasing numbers and ferocity. From August 24 to September 6 the raiders averaged more than a thousand planes a day.

The drill at Fighter Command Headquarters was a triumph of organization. It took a German bomber only six minutes to cross the Channel, so there was never a second to lose. Radar posts and the Observer Corps, watchers who had been trained in aircraft recognition, reported the approaching raiders. In the control room their course was plotted, the fighter stations alerted and the pilots directed to the enemy squadrons. From battered runways the British fighters roared off to intercept the bombers before they crossed the coast.

The fighter pilots lived constantly in a "ready for off" atmosphere. When a squadron was placed at readiness it could be air-borne in less than three minutes after the take-off signal. The pilots' lives were on the airfields, and they slept in huts a few yards from their aircraft. They wore flying kit all the time; their helmets and parachutes lay ready in the cockpits. Relays of mechanics kept the aircraft primed for action. They were determined that the planes should be worthy of the men who flew them.

The fighter pilots were under a tremendous strain, because they were so few. They flew sortie after sortie, sometimes six or seven a day; nothing seemed too much to demand of them. They outmatched the Luftwaffe in skill and daring.

As the German losses mounted, Göring had to send stronger fighter escorts to guard his bombers; but the R.A.F. roared in and ripped them to pieces.

The R.A.F. losses were heavy too: in ten days during August a hundred and fifty-four fighter pilots were killed or seriously wounded. For the first time, though, the R.A.F. was fighting in its own skies. If pilots had to bail out they landed among friends and were back in the battle in a few hours.

The first fighter pilot to win a V.C. (Victoria Cross), the highest British award for bravery, was Flight Lieutenant Nicholson. His was typical of many acts of courage. His Hurricane was hit by four cannon shells. Two struck him and wounded him severely; then one struck the reserve gasoline tank, and he was badly burned by the flames. As he was preparing to bail out he saw a Messerschmitt and thought that he could destroy it. Disregarding pain and danger, he attacked, using up the precious time when he could have escaped. He brought down the Messerschmitt before he bailed out.

The gallantry of the men was upheld by the women of the Women's Auxiliary Air Force (WAAF). They carried out duties on air stations during grueling raids, with no thought of danger. At the Biggin Hill fighter station in Kent, which was repeatedly bombed, Sergeant Joan Mortimer remained at her post in a very heavy raid, with bombs falling around her. Before the All Clear sounded she went out to the runway and planted red flags around the craters containing unexploded bombs, to warn the pilots.

All summer Bomber Command of the R.A.F. harassed concentrations of German invasion barges along the French and Belgian coast, and bombed railways which carried German supplies. Hamm, Germany's biggest marshaling yard, came into the news, for the trains which passed through it, laden with guns, fuel, and ammunition, made important targets. The R.A.F. called this regular bombing raid the Hamm and Egg Run ("egg" being slang for a bomb).

Despite the raids the concentration of invasion craft grew. At the beginning of September preparations appeared to have reached a climax. Throughout Britain all the armed forces were alerted with the signal "Invasion Imminent." But it was postponed. Hitler dared not take the chance, and the German High Command had to face the facts: the R.A.F. was beating the Luftwaffe out of the skies; it was getting too late in the season to count on smooth seas for the invasion fleet; and British bombing had upset supply lines.

On September 15 the Luftwaffe staged their famous last massed daylight raid. By that time the R.A.F. was very tired — but triumphant.

This was the fiercest fight of all. Wave after wave of bombers was hurled against southeast England on this sunny Sunday, and many reached the London area. The roar of aircraft and the crash of falling bombs continued through the day. High up, out of sight, the fighters found the enemy and drove them down. The dazzling blue of the sky was cut by white vapor trails and smeared with the dark spirals of falling aircraft. In London newsboys chalked up the score for the waiting crowds. By evening the Battle of Britain was over, for when Göring counted up his losses, he abandoned the policy of daylight bombing and turned to raiding London by night.

The fame of the little band of men who won the Battle of Britain will shine forever. Many of them died in the battle, and others who survived it did not live to see the final victory they had given so much to gain.

In Winston Churchill's words: "Never in the field of human conflict was so much owed by so many to so few."

9

The Blitz

THE BATTLE OF BRITAIN was a grave setback for Nazi Germany. It was Hitler's first defeat. The Luftwaffe was losing far more crews and aircraft than it could afford. Britain was gaining strength in the organized manufacture of war material, and America was coming to her aid. The 1940 invasion was off.

Hitler tried to cover it up by telling the German people that night attacks on London and other industrial cities would be "the knockout blow," following on the somber pattern of Warsaw and Rotterdam. The city at the heart of the British Empire was to be battered into subjection. But Göring did not allow either for the immensity of his target or the spirit of the people. Cockneys christened his attack the "blitz," borrowing part of the German word *Blitzkrieg*, with its reference to a lightning attack.

The Luftwaffe succeeded in inflicting deep scars

on the capital, crippling its industries, slaughtering and maiming its citizens. But the city lived on, for the bombing merely hardened the resolve and sharpened the loathing of the British people.

In Germany also, during the next five years, as the weight of Allied retaliation began to fall on one city after another, the population faced agony and devastation with sullen determination.

On September 7 the blitz opened with a heavy attack on the London docks. The Luftwaffe dropped thousands of incendiary bombs by day followed by high explosive bombs that night. Miles of warehouses along the Thames River were left ablaze. In Woolwich Arsenal firemen could not fight the flames through the barrage of exploding ammunition. In the great warehouses the flames were fed by thousands of tons of tea, sugar, wheat, and oil. Rum and paint formed molten streams sizzling into the Thames. The stench of burning rubber carried for fifty miles. The closely packed rows of little houses around the docks had their first deadly baptism of fire.

From that day until Christmas the Luftwaffe returned almost every night. The London air raid sirens wailed each evening at dusk, closely followed by the sinister drone of the approaching bombers. Often the All Clear sounded only with the dawn, and then weary Londoners emerged from their shelters to view the ugly scene of desolation.

King George VI and Queen Elizabeth lived calmly on at Buckingham Palace through the bombing, sharing the sorrows of other Londoners. They visited bombed-out areas and talked to the people. So did Winston Churchill, and wherever he went he was welcomed with his two-finger symbol — the "V for victory" sign.

No part of London escaped the bombing. Buckingham Palace was hit three times, and the Chamber of the House of Commons was wrecked. Hospitals and schools, factories and railways, shops and offices and above all the homes of the people came under fire.

The enemy favored moonlit nights. The terms "Harvest Moon" and "Hunter's Moon" were out of date, and people spoke grimly of "Bomber's Moon." At first it seemed to Londoners as if no one was hitting back. After a long night filled with the sickening roar of exploding bombs, they would read next day of "one enemy aircraft destroyed." Later the comforting clatter of antiaircraft guns mingled with the bombing. Later still, when the British night fighters got going, the Luftwaffe pilots were not so fond of the moon.

The German bombers flew on a radio beam, transmitted from the Continent, which led them to the target. The system was not entirely accurate, but it was good enough to guide them to a large city, where they were almost sure to hit something. British scientists learned to jam these beams, turning them away from the target. Decoy fires were lighted several miles away from a town to confuse the enemy. In this way a raid aimed at Derby was directed to a lonely moor, with the result that a large enemy bomber force killed two cows and two chickens instead of hitting the Rolls Royce aircraft-engine plant.

Londoners learned to live with the bombing. Most of them sent their children to safety areas. Then they settled down to an unreal kind of life, living from day to day, always in the shadow of danger. Nothing had much point except winning the war.

People slept in all kinds of shelters. In Stepney, near the London docks, where the bombing was bad, they crowded into huge arches under a railroad warehouse. "Meet you under the Arches" became a nightly greeting; at one time eight thousand people sheltered there. In the early days of the blitz they had no sanitation, no heating, no bunks, and very little lighting. Sitting or lying miserably on any bedding they had been able to carry in, they waited for the dawn.

As evening came crowds poured into the subway stations and slept on the platforms, undisturbed by passing trains. It seemed peaceful because there were much worse sounds overhead, and underground people could seldom hear the bombs. Above all, they did not want to be alone.

Later the shelters were improved by public authority; in the bigger ones canteens, lavatories, bunks, and even night club shows and movies were provided. Shelter life became a thing of its own.

The full story of the blitz can never be told. It

is made up of thousands of acts of bravery and neighborly devotion. Through their fear and suffering the people of the bombed cities built up a wonderful comradeship. They housed and clothed the "bombed outs" who had lost their homes; they shared their rations and comforted one another. Most people clung stubbornly to their own locality. Even when they had been bombed out several times they refused to go to the country.

Men and women kept on with their jobs. It seemed the only way to beat the Nazis. If they lost their homes during the night, in the morning they trudged off to work through the rubbish and splintered glass, wondering if the office or factory was still there, and hoping the gas mains had not been hit, so they could have a hot meal and a cup of tea. Postmen collected letters from mailboxes covered with debris, and milk and newspapers arrived as a matter of course on doorsteps where there were no doors.

The whole army of Civil Defense workers fought in the Battle of the Blitz. The Fire Service, doctors, policemen, ambulance drivers, rescue squads, and air raid wardens were up most of every night. When an incident was reported a control center sent out help. Usually the air raid warden was already on the spot. King George VI issued the George Medal, a special medal for conspicuous gallantry to which civilians were entitled. It was earned many times.

In the first twenty-two days of the blitz the Fire Service fought ten thousand fires, sometimes over a thousand in one night. The firemen were always in danger because the first bombers dropped incendiaries to lead the way for the next wave, bearing high explosives, to the same target. Broken mains were the firemen's chief foe, for the water would rush in torrents through the streets, and there would be no pressure for the hoses.

The bombing of the heart of London took place on December 29, 1940. The area around St. Paul's Cathedral was saturated with incendiaries. They rained down on the old buildings, and in half an hour, fanned by a gentle breeze, the whole section was a sea of leaping flames. The sky over London was brighter than at noon, and to the stunned crowds watching from across the river it seemed as though nothing could be saved. When at last the fires were under control and St. Paul's still stood, towering above the smoldering ruins, people marveled. It was a symbol of survival. Next day crowds of smoke-grimed people filed slowly along the narrow, roped-off lanes, through the blackened stones, in thankful silence.

By November it was obvious that London had cheated the Luftwaffe of its triumph, for damage was patched up from raid to raid, business went on and civilian morale was high. So Göring started a series of attacks on industrial cities throughout Britain. In Coventry, which was the first victim, damage to industry was considerable, and the center of the city was blotted out; only the cathedral spire rose starkly above the gutted shell — an emblem of defiance. Many other cities shared a similar fate. Production dropped and exhaustion rose, as one after another met the ordeal.

The bombing of Britain was a challenge to ordinary people to play their part. No one liked it, but they set their teeth and stuck it out. Years later most people remember not the fear, but the dirt and weariness. They remember too the waste and cruelty of war.

Though early in 1941 the raids came less often, they increased in viciousness. Then in the spring they petered out, and British cities were to enjoy a long spell of quiet. The policy of mass bombing had failed to defeat Britain, and the Luftwaffe turned east to darken the skies over Russia, Germany's own ally.

10

The Battle of the Atlantic

This CHAPTER TELLS the story of the endurance and limitless courage of the men who fought in the Battle of the Atlantic. It tells the tale of some of the big ships and of the ceaseless, valiant struggle of the little ships.

Until America entered the war, the task of keeping open the long, stormy sea lanes was shared by the navies, merchant navies, and air forces of Britain and Canada. They set out day after day, year after year, through gales, mine-infested waters, and hostile skies, constantly aware of the perils surrounding them, but never giving in.

Battleships and cruisers, submarines and destroyers, queenly passenger liners and snub-nosed trawlers, heavy-laden tankers wallowing in the deep troughs of the Atlantic, corvettes that tossed like corks in the slightest storm — they all played a part in bringing home the precious cargoes.

It was a battle for Britain's survival; everything

depended on it. It is impossible on so small an island to produce enough for fifty million people to live on, let alone fight with. The ships bearing food for the people, oil for the tanks and planes, and supplies for the factories had to be gotten through. If Hitler could win the Battle of the Atlantic, all his other battles would be easy.

In Germany the situation was different. Since many surrounding countries had been overpowered by German forces, most of the essential supplies came in overland. The anxiety about the safe passage of the Swedish iron ore had been settled by the conquest of Norway. Each conquered country was robbed for Nazi needs. There were still some gaps, but German scientists were working hard to fill them. Oil was produced from coal, and synthetic rubber had been invented. The German Navy was designed to sink enemy cargoes rather than to protect its own.

On paper, at the start of the war, the British Navy looked far stronger than the German Navy. Actually, because Britain had not armed between the wars, many of her battleships were left over from the First World War, and few of her ships were as fast or well armed as their German opposite numbers.

Hitler had built up the German Navy with well-designed modern craft. Although the Versailles Treaty limited the size of German warships, skillful designers crammed them with big guns and heavy armor. Ships which were supposed to be cruisers, like the *Graf Spee* and the *Admiral Scheer*, were in fact far more powerful, and were called "pocket battleships." By 1939 the Nazis were building two tremendous battleships, the *Bismarck* and the *Tirpitz*, five new cruisers, and as many submarines as they could turn out.

Both the British and German navies laid mine fields. By international law the areas had to be declared, so that the enemy entered them at his own risk. The waters off the east coast of Britain and the Straits of Dover were heavily mined, with clear routes secretly charted for British shipping.

Early in the war the Germans scored a big success with their newly invented magnetic mine. Up till then all mines had been exploded by contact, and they remained harmless unless a ship hit them. The magnetic mines exploded when a ship merely came within a certain distance of them. Ordinary mines were swept up in nets by mine sweepers which worked continually, clearing safe passages. But the magnetic mines could not be swept up because they exploded first, and sank the mine sweepers.

At one time the huge Port of London was almost closed because the seagoing channels were blocked with magnetic mines, which were dropped at night by parachute from German aircraft. They were designed to drift just below the surface.

When things looked very bad the British had a stroke of good luck. A magnetic mine fell on the soft mud flats at Shoeburyness, on the east coast of

England, without exploding. With infinite patience and bravery Lieutenant Commander Ouvry dissected the mine. Every movement might well have been his last. Step by step, he took the mine to pieces and discovered the secret. He found that magnetic mines were exploded by a change of magnetism, brought about by the near presence of a steel hull.

With this knowledge British scientists worked out ways to beat the magnetic mine. Ships were fitted with enormous metallic coils through which an electric current was passed, which neutralized the magnetic effect of the ship's hull. A way was also found to explode the mines harmlessly. But while the secret lasted the magnetic mines had given a lot of trouble.

After the fall of France, Germany held the whole coast line of Europe from the northern tip of Norway to the southwestern tip of France at the Spanish frontier, with a string of fine harbors thrown in. Ships could be based at Narvik in the north, Trondheim and Bergen in central Norway, Kiel and Wilhelmshaven in Germany, Brest, Cherbourg, and St. Nazaire in France.

From any of these ports they could launch an attack on Allied shipping. They could send out armed raiders, like the *Graf Spee* or the *Admiral Scheer,* and groups of submarines to hunt in packs. Long-range aircraft could take off from dozens of airfields, loaded with mines, bombs, or torpedoes. The British Admiralty tried hard to spot the movements of the German battle fleet by R.A.F. reconnaissance, but often the warships stole out at night or under cover of low cloud, and were lost in the vast oceans.

Just west of the British Isles lies an area of the Atlantic Ocean known as the Western Approaches. Shipping laden with cargoes from all over the world must cross these waters to reach Britain. So it was in this critical area that a great part of the Atlantic War was waged.

Coastal Command of the R.A.F. was formed to work with the Navy. The aircraft patrolled the sea routes, attacked U-boats and searched for armed raiders.

From the beginning of the war Allied shipping traveled in convoy, grouped together for safety and escorted by warships. There were appalling difficulties. The cargo ships came from all over the world; the enemy was always waiting to pounce; and there were not enough Allied warships to go around.

Convoys sailed at secretly arranged times from fixed assembly points, where the merchant ships would gather and wait for their escorts. Sometimes a convoy contained as many as sixty ships, and the slowest vessel always set the pace.

The strength of the escort varied, since destroyers and corvettes were scarce. Through American generosity Britain received fifty destroyers for the escort fleet, but there still were not enough to cover all the shipping routes.

The Germans sent long-range Focke-Wulf bombers — Condors — to join the battle. The U-boats hunted in groups called "wolf packs." A Condor or a single U-boat would sight a convoy and shadow it, signaling for the pack to close in for the kill. Then, under cover of darkness, the U-boats would launch repeated massed attacks with frightening success.

In the Atlantic the escorts took the convoys outbound from Britain or Canada to a given point and then sent them on their way. Then they waited to bring an incoming convoy home. Once the merchant ships were off on their own they had to defend themselves as best they could. Against an armed raider or a U-boat their only hope was to scatter; but against low-flying aircraft they stood a chance if they were provided with good antiaircraft guns.

There was an acute shortage of guns in the early days of the war. Even the old machine guns left over from the First World War had been dug out of storage and were being used. The Admiralty scoured the arms depots and factories and tried to borrow from the Army, but in 1940, with the Germans massing for the invasion of Britain, the Army did not have enough for its own needs. Some ships sailed with kites and balloons in tow, hoping to deter low-flying aircraft; and some even carried ordinary fireworks, intending to let them off in a crisis to discourage a low-level attack. But the crews were anxious to put up a fight for their ships and their lives, and they demanded decent weapons. As production gradually increased they got them.

The Halifax convoys became famous. Ships from the Americas would assemble in the Canadian port of Halifax in Nova Scotia. Heavily laden, they sailed doggedly in all weather in the face of ferocious enemy attack, the captains prepared to fight their cargoes through at any cost.

The fast, modern merchant ships sailed alone, zigzagging as they went to outwit the U-boats. The slower ships trudged along in convoy, protected whenever possible by the Canadian and British navies.

German U-boats and armed raiders would lie in wait for the Halifax convoys. They preferred to sink the ships when they were approaching Britain, so that they could destroy the cargoes too.

In October 1940 the pocket battleship *Admiral Scheer* was completed. She was sent off at once to the Western Approaches to smash the convoys. She had not long to wait, for on November 3 a convoy of thirty-seven ships hove in sight, escorted only by one armed merchant cruiser, the *Jarvis Bay*, under Captain Fegen.

It was clear to Captain Fegen that, with a few old six-inch guns, his ship did not stand a chance in battle against the pocket battleship. He knew, too, that his only hope of saving the convoy was to engage the enemy long enough to give the ships time to scatter.

Darkness was approaching, and if the *Admiral Scheer* could be held off for an hour the whole convoy might escape. So the *Jarvis Bay*, with its guns blazing, closed in to draw the enemy fire. Fighting against hopeless odds Captain Fegen kept his ship in action for an hour and ten minutes until every gun was silenced and she was a flaming wreck.

When the fight was over the *Admiral Scheer* turned to the convoy, but by this time dusk had fallen and the ships had dispersed. She was able to find and attack only five of the thirty-seven. Of these the tanker *San Demetrio* was set on fire, and the signal was given to abandon ship. Part of her crew drifted all night in an open boat. The next day they found the *San Demetrio*, still burning, but afloat. They boarded her, and despite the risk of explosion they put out the fire. With no navigational aids but the sun and stars, they brought her safely in with her precious cargo.

Captain Fegen went down with his ship and was awarded the V.C. for his gallant action. Through the sacrifice of the *Jarvis Bay* thirty-three ships came safely to port.

11

American Lend-Lease
and the Grand Alliance

IN HER HOUR of need Britain found a great war
leader; so did the United States.

President Franklin D. Roosevelt was from the first
day of the war wholeheartedly pro-British and anti-
Nazi. He knew that the days were past when Americans could sit back and let other nations fight for
the freedom of the English-speaking world. He saw
that if Britain did not get the help she so desperately needed the tide of Nazi conquest would sweep
over the Atlantic and swamp America.

President Roosevelt was a very remarkable man.
He was stricken with infantile paralysis at the beginning of his political career; but, in spite of his
infirmity, he went on to win his country's highest
office. He is the only man ever to have been elected
President of the United States four times. He fought

each election campaign from a wheel chair and was triumphantly returned for his third term in November 1940, at the height of the crisis in European affairs.

Winston Churchill had become Prime Minister six months earlier, and a powerful partnership began to take shape. The basis of Roosevelt's policy was "all aid to Britain short of war," but it took time to convince some of the American people of this.

In January 1941 he said to Congress: "We know that enduring peace cannot be bought at the cost of other people's freedom."

And to Britain and the Commonwealth: "We Americans are vitally concerned in your defense and freedom. We are putting forth our energies, our resources, and our organizing powers to give you the strength to regain and maintain a free world. We shall send you in ever-increasing numbers, ships, planes, tanks, guns. This is our purpose and our pledge."

The vast storehouse of American production had almost everything that Britain lacked to carry on the war — steel and ships, guns and ammunition, tanks and tractors, food for the people, and fuel for the machines.

America was to become what Roosevelt called "the arsenal of the democracies."

The American Government forbade its ships to enter the war zone, for fear of a sinking which might bring the United States into the war. So the goods had to be fetched and carried by British ships and the merchantmen of other countries. Many valuable cargoes were sunk in the Atlantic, and more strongly armed escorts were needed to get the ships safely through. When America decided to turn over to Britain her fifty destroyers they were a godsend.

The next big steppingstone across the Atlantic was laid in March 1941 when the Lend-Lease Act was passed by Congress. At the outbreak of war Britain had 4.5 billion dollars in gold and investments in America. By January 1941 she had spent it all on food and arms, and she had no more credit. So the governments got together, and Britain leased to America naval bases in the Caribbean Sea. These would be used for American defense in time of war. In return, the British Government was allowed to place orders in America for weapons and supplies which they could not pay for in hard cash. To meet the orders American industry turned from peace to war. Shipyards and factories, steel mills and oil wells joined the arms race against Germany.

In June 1941 Germany attacked Russia. America was still at peace, but she was drawing closer to Britain all the time. Huge problems faced both nations; for years their leaders had written to each other, now it was vital that they should meet.

It would have been against the wishes of the American people for President Roosevelt to go to Britain at the height of a war, so it was arranged that Winston Churchill should cross the Atlantic in great secrecy and meet him in some lonely spot.

Every precaution was taken to conceal the journey from the Germans, for Hitler would have sent out every U-boat and surface raider to destroy his enemy. Churchill sailed with his staff in the new battleship *Prince of Wales* and on August 9, 1941, arrived safely at Placentia Bay in Newfoundland, where the President awaited him.

It was a momentous meeting. Britain was fighting for her life, and the mighty strength of America had not yet been wholly cast into the battle. But the future Grand Alliance was taking shape, and the Stars and Stripes flew side by side with the Union Jack when President Roosevelt came on board the *Prince of Wales* for church services on Sunday. Winston Churchill, in his *History of World War II*, tells how the President stood while "God Save the King" was sung; and how the Prime Minister himself chose the hymns: "For Those in Peril on the Sea," "Onward Christian Soldiers," and "O God Our Help in Ages Past." Both men knew that the struggle for freedom must be long and hard.

The whole range of Anglo-American unity was discussed, and a statement made for all the world to read — the Atlantic Charter. It set out the aims of the United States and the British Commonwealth; it was a pledge of their united faith in freedom.

Winston Churchill returned to London on August 18, 1941. By the end of that year the United States was at war, and the proud battleship *Prince of Wales*, with her captain and many of her gallant crew, had perished.

12

War in the Libyan Desert

IN THE AUTUMN of 1940, when the Battle of Britain was over, fighting flared up in a new area. The thunder of battle rolled from Britain to the shores of the Mediterranean.

Hitler and Mussolini were on the warpath together, although they were jealous and distrustful of each other. Their partnership was born of greed and nourished on violence.

In May 1940, when the Nazi divisions were sweeping across Europe, Mussolini had been frantic. His plans had gone wrong; he was not ready for war, his armed forces were not up to strength, the Italian people had not been properly educated to the idea, and his finances were shaky. But with the French Army routed and the B.E.F. being pushed into the sea, Allied defeat seemed inevitable. Mussolini simply did not dare to leave Hitler alone in his triumph. Moreover, he could not bear to miss the booty after the victory.

The conquest of Egypt was Mussolini's crowning ambition. He craved the riches of the Nile Delta, the cities of Cairo and Alexandria and control of the Suez Canal. He dreamed of the revival of the Roman Empire with the Duce a demigod at its head. In the autumn of 1940 Britain was so hard pressed on all sides that Mussolini thought that his golden opportunity had come to steal a march on Egypt. He hoped that the British Empire was crumbling and the ill-equipped Italian Army would get through without much fighting.

In the center of the North African coast line, adjoining Egypt, was Libya, Italy's largest colony. This was well garrisoned with Italian troops. But Egypt had a British garrison, for Britain had a treaty with Egypt which allowed her to keep troops there to protect the interests of both Great Britain and Egypt.

In the summer of 1940, when General Graziani was mustering the Italian armies on the Egyptian frontier, General Wavell commanded the British armies in the Middle East and Air Marshal Longmore, the R.A.F. Both British commanders were dismally short of men and equipment.

Desert warfare has a character of its own. Armies have to learn the ways of the desert before they can tackle the enemy. The desert is like an ocean — there are few landmarks, and men must navigate by compass or the stars.

The pattern of living and the pace of fighting

are dictated by the country itself, and the rules are always changing. The desert contributes nothing either to support life or to fight with. An army must carry supplies for all its needs.

In summer the Libyan Desert is very hot during the day and cold at night. In winter it is bitterly cold, and torrential rains turn the few roads and tracks into rivers of mud. The country varies from the Libyan "sand sea," which is a large expanse of soft, shifting sands, almost untracked, to the Qattara Depression, where tiers of jagged cliffs rise out of sandy clefts to form an impassable barrier for a hundred and fifty miles.

Most of the desert surface is studded with boulders, little outcrops of rock and patches of stunted scrub. Snakes and scorpions lurk under the stones, and flies are constant pests. There is little shade from the heat or shelter from the wind.

But the greatest snag is the sand itself. It seeps in everywhere, and men grow to loathe it. In summer the hot khamsin wind blows, sometimes for days on end, bringing a sandstorm in its wake. The dense swirling clouds hold up transport and blot out the landscape. The fine dust coats everything and clogs machines. Grit filters into food and wounds and tempers. Life becomes intolerable. The desert is a hard master.

Reports filtered through the lines that Italian morale was low, and General Wavell planned to reduce it further. Unable to employ large forces, he sent out small, well-trained units to harass the enemy. They made short, sharp attacks on camps and outposts, shot the sentries and often made off with a few prisoners before the Italians knew what was happening.

By December 1940 the British troops had gained useful desert experience, and the Seventh Armored Division, composed of some of the best units in the army, was ready to strike.

General Wavell drew up a plan so secret that it was never put down on paper until the final orders were given. A compact armored force was to penetrate enemy positions, bypass their forward camps, and then swing up to the coast, cutting their communications. It was to be a raid, possibly widening into an offensive; and it worked better than the British command had dared to hope. The R.A.F. plastered the enemy airfields in front of the advancing armor and kept the Italian Air Force out of the air.

The enemy in Nibeiwa camp was taken by surprise and surrounded. Reinforcements arrived and put up some resistance, but the Italian officers were unskilled in desert tactics, and the men soon lost heart. Thousands surrendered, and, with their officers, marched away into captivity, leaving masses of stores and equipment, disordered but intact.

Alan Moorehead, one of the war correspondents with the forward British troops, gives a most graphic account of Italian camp life. The officers lived like lords. They had tried to shut out the rigors of the desert with a curtain of luxury. Their beds were made up with clean linen; their fine uniforms with flowing blue cloaks, sashes, and tassels would have adorned a parade ground; their dressing tables were decked with silver-backed brushes and bottles of scent. The canteens were stocked with a selection of the choicest food and wine; and each Italian soldier had his own little *espresso* coffee machine.

The raid turned into an orderly pursuit, and the Italian withdrawal into a massed retreat. As the armies moved westward along the coastal strip, where the only road was, all the names that were to become so familiar during the next few years appeared in the news: Sidi Barrani, Buq Buq, Sollum, with its sheer cliff topped by Halfaya (Hellfire) Pass, Bardia, Tobruk, Gazala and Derna. They fell one by one to the Seventh Armored Division, which later gained fame and glory under the nickname "Desert Rats," and to the Australian and Indian divisions which together led the advance.

Sharp orders came through from Mussolini for his armies to stand and fight. They obediently stood and fought at intervals along the route, but by and large the retreat continued.

General O'Connor, commanding the army in the field, relentlessly pressed on, never allowing the disorganized columns to re-form.

As the British pushed west and their lines of communication lengthened, the problem of maintenance and supply grew. Captured stores and dumps yielded some food and fuel, and Italian lorries were put into service; but the tank divisions had to take the risk of outrunning their supplies and finding themselves suddenly stranded and defenseless. Every gallon of fuel counted. Always the advancing army passed long lines of Italian prisoners streaming toward Egypt.

The town of Bengasi stands on a headland, and the area was jammed with a wild confusion of Italian troops and vehicles. With skill and daring, General O'Connor sent the Seventh Armored Division

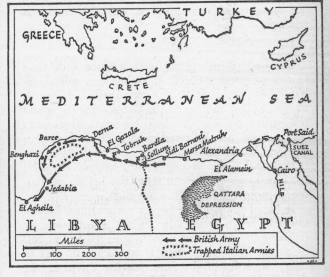

Defeat of the Italian Desert Army, February 1941

on an inland sweep to cut off the routed armies.
It meant leaving the coastal road to travel through
desert wastes in enemy country. As the vast con-
glomeration of the Italian armies rolled back in
chaos they found the British forces blocking their
path. They were hemmed in, and hardly a man or
vehicle escaped.

After ten weeks of continuous action a British
force of two divisions had advanced seven hundred
miles and destroyed an army of ten divisions. The
men were exhausted and their vehicles were worn
out and broken down; but it was a tremendous
triumph.

The tired British forces were granted little time
to rest on their success. Mussolini had seized Albania, bordering on Greece, on April 7, 1939. Although Mussolini assured the Greeks that he would
not harm them, they doubted his word. Mussolini's
"assurances" had followed such a familiar pattern
of Nazi-Fascist behavior that it inspired little faith
in the mind of the Greeks. Accordingly, on April 13,
the Greeks accepted with relief the British guarantee to protect them from aggression.

In October 1940, true to totalitarian form, Mussolini attacked Greece. She instantly appealed for
British aid. Britain was heavily engaged in the battle in the Western Desert. It was a fearful risk to
take troops out of the lines, leaving Egypt lightly
defended against large Italian forces. But it was the

policy of the British Government to fight for freedom wherever they could find allies, and the Greek
Army, though small, was fighting sturdily. So units
of British, Australian, and New Zealand forces were
landed in Greece and on the Greek island of Crete,
and a few precious aircraft were moved over from
Egypt.

The Greeks put up a far stronger resistance than
the Italians expected and held them at bay all winter. In the spring, however, Hitler decided to rescue
his blundering partner. On April 6 German troops
crossed the Greek frontier, and on April 24 the
Greek Army surrendered. The British and Commonwealth forces were faced with an evacuation on the
lines of Dunkirk, but far from home and with little
air support.

They crossed from the Greek mainland to the
island of Crete and took up a stand. The battle that
followed was fought with intense fury. The Germans brought in waves of parachute troops. These
were the elite of the German Army, fanatical Nazis
picked for their passionate devotion to the Führer.
They had been cheated of the triumph of landing
in Britain, and now their time had come. Their
losses were enormous, but for ten days the supply
never faltered.

The Commonwealth and Greek forces in Crete
were under the command of the New Zealander,
General Freyberg. His unsurpassed gallantry was a
legend and an inspiration to his men. In World
War I he had won the V.C. and a D.S.O. with two

bars. He had been wounded repeatedly, and fought dauntlessly wherever he met the enemy.

In Crete the forces under him were worthy of his leadership. They held on until General Freyberg himself ordered a retreat. Under murderous fire, with no respite or hope of reinforcement, they fought until they had nothing left to fight with. Outnumbered, exhausted, and hungry, by sheer courage they crippled the crack Nazi air-borne division so severely that it never again appeared in battle.

In the end the Navy, with heavy loss, took off about half the heroic garrison. The rest had been killed or driven into hiding in the mountains.

The Yugoslav Government had no choice but to sign, on March 25, 1941, an agreement with the Axis to keep their country out of war.

When the Yugoslav people heard of the pact there was a surge of anti-German feeling. On March 27, an uprising, led by officers of the Yugoslav air force, compelled the government to resign. Prince Paul left the country.

Although the young king was held in high esteem as a symbol of independence, and the country was swept with patriotic feeling, the new government decided to abide by the pact signed by the former government a few days earlier.

But this did not appease Hitler. He was incensed at the Yugoslavs for their anti-German uprising. He swore to avenge the insult. On April 6, the day his armies invaded Greece, they also marched into Yugoslavia.

Young Peter escaped to England, but resistance to the Nazis soon began, first under a Yugoslav Army officer named Mikhailovitch — and later under a 49-year-old Yugoslav Communist named Josip Broz Tito.

At the same time, in what Hitler called "Operation Punishment," the Luftwaffe attacked Belgrade, the Yugoslav capital. For three days without pause the bombers blasted the city, flying at rooftop level. It was reduced to a smoking tomb, and seventeen thousand people died in the ruins. There was no possible object in the massacre except revenge. The Yugoslav Army had not been mobilized, and the Germans could have captured the country almost without bloodshed.

Hitler had been bent on bringing Yugoslavia into the Axis orbit for some time. The country was made up of three ethnic groups, the Serbs, the Croats, and the Slovenes. The country was ruled, in effect, by the chief regent, Prince Paul, on behalf of King Peter II, who was underage.

In March 1941, the country was surrounded by enemies. In the west was Fascist Italy, hungering for Yugoslav territory. Toward the north and to the east was Nazi Germany and her old foes, Hungary and Bulgaria. To the south, Italy occupied Albania. At the same time, German troops were moving through Rumania and Bulgaria to rescue their

Italian ally who was being mauled by the Greeks.

The Germans began to pressure the Yugoslavs to join the Axis. The Yugoslavs, in turn, asked the British what help they could expect from them if the Germans invaded Yugoslavia. The British, fighting desperately in Africa and committed to help the Greeks, could not pledge to defend Yugoslavia in case of a German invasion.

Even as the Germans were invading Yugoslavia and dropping paratroopers into Greece to bail out their Italian ally, they were also going to Italy's rescue in the Western Desert.

Hitler had tried to ignore the North African campaign. He was planning to invade Russia; he despised Italian inefficiency; and he was not prepared to bolster up Mussolini's tottering army with modern German arms. However, he was advised by the German High Command that if nothing was done to stiffen up resistance, the Italian armies would be pushed out of Libya, and the German position in Tunisia, which they had taken from the French, would be endangered.

So Hitler agreed to send out an armored division, the Deutsche Afrika Korps. In command was General Erwin Rommel, who had so successfully led the Panzer divisions across the Meuse and on to victory in France. On February 11 Marshal Graziani resigned his command and left for Italy. On the following day Rommel arrived in North Africa to survey the shattered remains of the Italian armies.

The British Army also was in a bad way. First,

the ranks had been thinned in order to send help to Greece. Second, the Seventh Armored Division, which had formed the spearhead of the great advance, had been taken out of the line to rest the men after their strenuous campaign and to refit the tanks. The division had been replaced by troops with no desert experience, equipped with faulty tanks, some of which broke down before they ever reached the front line. Third, a great deal of energy and manpower was being used in supplying the Army with food and war material. Since Bengasi was under fire from the Luftwaffe the harbor was useless, and everything had to be brought from Tobruk — five hundred miles along one crowded, narrow coastal road.

Rommel wasted no time. On March 31, six weeks after his arrival in North Africa, he had gotten together enough troops and armor to launch an attack from his position at Agheila. The British forward troops were overrun by a superior tank force, and a withdrawal was ordered.

Then a misfortune occurred which affected the whole outcome of the battle. General O'Connor and General Neame were driving together to a new headquarters when they were surrounded in the dark by a German patrol and taken prisoner. This can well happen in the desert, where there are no clearly defined defenses; the front line is always changing, existing wherever fighting flares up. General O'Connor was a master of desert strategy, and it was hard to replace him.

Rommel surged on, outflanking the British armor, and in a few weeks the gains of the winter were lost. Only the vital harbor of Tobruk held out against German assault. An Australian division fought off fierce tank attacks and dug in; the men fortified an outer defense line and withstood enemy pressure from land, sea, and air. For months this isolated fortress behind Rommel's lines defied all his attempts to wipe it out. It was hazardously supplied by sea; mine layers stole in on moonless nights, landing food, ammunition, medical supplies, and even tanks.

Rommel halted his forces at Bardia, on the Egyptian frontier, and the British forces tried to reorganize in Egypt. It was at this gloomy time that the battles in Yugoslavia, Greece, and Crete drew to a disastrous close.

Since Hitler had started on his path of aggression he had seized fourteen countries: Austria, Czechoslovakia, Poland, Norway, Denmark, Holland, Belgium, Luxembourg, France, Yugoslavia, Rumania, Bulgaria, Hungary (by encirclement and occupation), and Greece (in partnership with Italy). Now he stood on the borders of Egypt.

13

The Russian Ordeal

On June 22, 1941, exactly a year after the French armistice was signed in the Forest of Compiègne, the world was astonished to hear that Germany had invaded her Communist ally, Russia.

When Hitler and Stalin had signed their nonaggression pact in 1939 they had agreed that under no circumstances whatsoever would they attack each other for at least ten years. They had also secretly agreed to carve up Poland, and, in return for a free hand in western Europe, Hitler promised not to interfere when Stalin seized Finland and the Baltic States.

It was an unholy alliance. Hitler had always intended to conquer Russia, but he was anxious to finish off France and Britain first. Stalin hated and feared Germany and hoped she would be weakened by the coming battles in the West. By signing the pact he too was simply playing for time, so that he could build up his own strength.

Stalin's conquests after 1939 did not compare with Hitler's in size, although he managed to snatch a slice of Poland, important bases in Finland, the three Baltic States (Estonia, Lithuania, and Latvia), and a piece of Rumania.

Yet Hitler, despite his resounding victories, was a disappointed man. He had not been able to subdue Britain, either by peace offers or by all-out air attack. She still stood, blocking the path of complete Nazi domination of Europe.

In the winter of 1940, when it became clear that the blitz on London would not make Britain surrender, Hitler grew impatient and decided to launch his attack on Russia anyway. Looking eastward he was sorely tempted by the wide Lebensraum — the rich wheat fields and granaries of the Ukraine and the oil flowing from the Caucasian wells. He had made up his mind after the Russian reverses in Finland that the Red Army was too feeble to give him much trouble. Hitler told himself and his generals that Britain was almost beaten and went ahead with his plans for "Operation Barbarossa" in the following spring.

The German people were going to be handed a new burden. Fresh sacrifices must be demanded of them, and the fact that Britain was still fighting had to be glossed over. So the Nazi propaganda machine came into action once more. Hitler decided he would tell the people that he had discovered Russia was on the point of making a secret agreement with Britain to attack Germany. He would pose as a savior delivering his homeland from the menace of communism. He had always hated communism, though in many ways it was similar to his own Nazi creed.

In conference with the German generals, Hitler issued his instructions. The ordinary rules of war would not apply to the Russians. The campaign was to be waged with unsparing brutality. The Nazi armies must live off the land, and no food need be left for the civilian population. The elderly or sick or the very young could be left to die, but any Russian who could be used as forced labor for the German war effort must be put to work at once.

Speaking to the German High Command just before the onslaught began, Hitler said: "When Barbarossa opens, the world will hold its breath." He reckoned that Russian resistance would last about two months, and that he could then turn west and deal the death blow to Britain.

When Britain and the Commonwealth learned that Hitler had attacked Soviet Russia they had mixed feelings about their new ally. It was true that Hitler was the main enemy and anyone fighting Hitler was welcome, but on the other hand Stalin had behaved shamefully. He had worked with Germany to destroy Poland and to acquire other peoples' territories. And communism was hateful to nations that believed in freedom.

Communism had grown out of the Russian Bolshevik revolution of 1917. At first, the peasants had risen in a body against the old way of life, welcoming their new leaders with wild enthusiasm. From feudal times until 1861 they had worked as serfs, tied to the estates of the great landowners who had the right to buy and sell them like slaves. Most of them were still very poor, never possessing a field of their own. Now they looked forward to being independent, for they believed that the revolution would even out money and distribute free land, so that all the Russian people would have an equal share.

In fact, when the Bolsheviks sacked the country and seized the estates, the peasants received their land. But their joy was short-lived, for a few years later the land was taken away by the Communist Party and made into huge collective farms. A million peasants starved to death, and those who protested were shot. The revolution had not brought freedom to the Russians; it had only changed their masters.

The Communist Party soon became all-powerful and ruled the Russian people harshly, led by dictators — first Lenin, then Stalin. Party members — "comrades" — laid down the law, and the ties of family, religion, and other loyalties were not allowed to interfere with the Party line. Freedom of speech and choice of action disappeared. The people were told what to do and what to think, and

German advance into Russia

any show of independence was stamped out with imprisonment, torture, and death.

At the time of the Nazi invasion Joseph Stalin had the modest-sounding title of General Secretary of the Communist Party of the Soviet Union. However, the extent of Stalin's power could not be measured by his title. He was a dictator as absolute and as autocratic as any Czar that ever ruled Russia. His word was law not only for the people of the Soviet Union but for the Communists who lived in countries far beyond the Russian borders.

In June 1941 Stalin found it difficult to believe that the Nazi troops, reported massing on the frontier, were going to strike. Up to the last moment Hitler had been friendly, and supplies of all kinds had been arriving in Russia regularly from German factories.

The attack followed the usual dictator pattern. No warning note was sounded. The Luftwaffe shot up the airfields, destroying most of the Soviet aircraft on the ground; then the armies moved in. From the Arctic Circle to the Black Sea a hundred and fifty divisions, including nineteen armored and twelve motorized, rolled across the frontier. The Finns in the north joined the German armies and attacked Leningrad; and in the south the Rumanian Army marched against Russia, glad of the opportunity to avenge the Communist aggression.

Hitler established headquarters in East Prussia. Hidden in the depths of a forest, they were dramatically named the *Wolfschanze* (Wolf's Lair). From there he followed with intense interest every movement on the fronts.

The campaign opened well for the Nazis. The outnumbered Russian troops fell back, and in two weeks the German armies aiming at Moscow had advanced four hundred and fifty miles. Farther to the south, too, the invading forces moved fast; mile after mile of the golden harvest in the Ukraine had been beaten down and lay blackened and wasted.

But though the Russian armies had retreated all along the line, they had not been destroyed, for they had used the immense depth of their country to absorb the attack. They had given ground and had lost a great many men, killed or encircled by the German armored forces, but a steady stream of Russian reserves flowed into the gaps.

It became clear to the Nazi generals very early in the campaign that Hitler had misjudged the Russian fighting strength. The German armies were deep in enemy territory, and the land between the battle front and their bases was occupied by a violently hostile people who were making life as dangerous and difficult as possible for the invaders.

On July 3 Stalin in an Order of the Day announced his "scorched earth" policy. He ordered that if the Red Army were forced back, everything behind it must be destroyed; even at the cost of starvation for the Russian people, nothing was to be left for the Nazis. The command was zealously obeyed. Railways were wrecked, and not a single bridge was left standing. The Dnieper Dam, the great feat of Soviet engineering that had taken ten years to build, was blown up. Food stores were burned and tractors removed so that the soil could not be tilled for next year's crops. The advancing armies found a barren waste. Far from being able to live off the land, they could not even get a drink of water, because the wells had been poisoned.

By late August Moscow and Leningrad were still in Russian hands, and the German armies in the south were still hundreds of miles from the Caucasus oil fields. The two months which Hitler had set aside for the conquest of Russia had slipped away, and victory was far beyond his grasp.

Nevertheless, he sent for Mussolini to come to his headquarters and see how well things were going. Mussolini did not enjoy his visit, for he had no successes to display. Both in Libya and in Greece his armies had had to be rescued by the Germans.

Mussolini's only revenge for his humiliation was a personal one. Flying back from a tour of the battle front in Hitler's private aircraft, he insisted on taking over the controls. Though very nervous Hitler was powerless to prevent his guest's showing off his skill as a pilot, and it was reported that when they landed safely his relief was obvious.

The autumn rains fell, and the Russian roads that had been churned up into clouds of dust during the summer now turned to swamps. The Panzer divisions found themselves axle-deep in mud. But at the beginning of October, urged on by Hitler, the armies on the central front launched a fresh attack and reached a point only eighty miles from Moscow.

Hitler was jubilant. Speaking in Berlin he said: "Today I declare the enemy in the East has been struck down and will never rise again." A few days later the Nazi press made the startling statement that "the war in the East is over." It seemed to the German people that victory was just round the corner.

Then the Russian winter closed down over the front. Blizzards sweeping over these same plains around Moscow had brought disaster to Napoleon's armies in 1812. Hitler was too proud and too obstinate to learn by example.

He had not planned to fight a winter campaign, so his armies were not fitted out against the cold. They had no warm clothing, no sleeping bags, no heating, and no way of carrying supplies through the snow. The troops endured agony with frostbite, and thousands of them died of exposure.

A crisis broke out in the Nazi High Command. Field Marshal Brauchitsch, the Commander in Chief, advised that the German armies should withdraw, and he was supported by General Rundstedt in the south and General Guderian on the Moscow front. Hitler dismissed them all and took sole command of the Eastern Front. From that moment the strategy of the German armies started to go downhill; it was in the hands of a madman.

Hitler ordered the armies to stand and, if necessary, to freeze where they stood. It was a remarkable sign of the Führer's power that, despite a strong Russian counterattack on December 6 and the Arctic weather, the German troops did not retreat.

14

The Birth of the Eighth Army

IN JULY 1941 dread of war was deepening in America. It was a grim time for Britain, most of Europe, and the Middle East. Hitler was master of the Continental countries, Nazi armies were sweeping into Russia, and Rommel stood on the Egyptian frontier.

At this time important changes occurred in the British Middle East Command in Cairo. General Auchinleck came from India to succeed General Wavell; Air Marshal Tedder took over command of the R.A.F.; and General Cunningham was appointed to command the armies in the field. All the resources and energy of these commanders were directed to building up the damaged units of the British Army and Air Force in the Middle East before Rommel struck again.

About this time the Long-range Desert Group was formed. It was a small, well-trained striking force, designed to direct surprise attacks against remote enemy positions, causing alarm and confusion.

The Desert Group was made up of picked men, ready to accept severe discipline and hard living. They traveled light and camped in the desert for weeks on end. Rations were sparse, and each man was limited to a single cup of water night and morning.

"Butcher" Graziani, who had been Italian Governor of eastern Libya before the war, had earned that title through his barbaric dealings with the Senusi Arabs. They are a religious sect, mostly shepherds, ranging the desert with their flocks — a primitive people opposed to progress and Italian interference. Graziani captured their chieftains, took them up in an airplane, bound in chains, and flung them out over their native city of Kufara, to be dashed to death before the eyes of their own people. So in Libya the British Desert Group was hailed as liberator by the Senusi, who did all they could to help them. It was a chance to throw off the hated Italian yoke.

All through the summer of 1941 both General Auchinleck and General Rommel were writing home for reinforcements. But Hitler needed all the tanks and guns he could lay hands on to make up his losses on the Russian front, and British and American factories were not yet geared to full production. However, by autumn lend-lease was beginning to tell, and General Auchinleck and Air Marshal Tedder had assembled enough strength to attack.

On November 18, 1941, the British and Commonwealth forces, now called the Eighth Army, crossed the Libyan frontier under General Cunningham with all the armor that they could command.

Rommel was taken by surprise. He was in Rome, but flew at once to the front. He flung the entire might of the Afrika Korps against the Eighth Army.

In the first leap the Eighth Army reached a point near Tobruk, and there they met the full weight of the enemy armor.

The tanks joined battle. The Germans had far stronger firepower, but the British were rallied again and again under the gallant leadership of Brigadier Jock Campbell. Always in the forefront of the battle, he led his tanks like cavalry charges. Ignoring the danger and the odds, he fought with his men, manning their guns when they fell beside him. "Jock's Columns" inflicted heavy loss on the enemy, and Brigadier Campbell was awarded the V.C.

The Eighth Army losses were severe, and they lacked the tank-recovery service by which the Germans collected their damaged tanks and repaired them rapidly for the next battle.

Near Tobruk the New Zealand division fought magnificently under their brilliant commander General Freyberg. They formed a human barrier with fixed bayonets, and held the coastal ridge against the enemy in hand-to-hand fighting, with fearful casualties.

General Rommel flung out a strong armored

spearhead to sever the Eighth Army from its supply base. The fate of Egypt hung in the balance. The maneuver was blocked by the personal intervention of General Auchinleck, who flew from Cairo to the battle front to save the situation, and by the superb defense of the R.A.F., which blasted the enemy armor and brought it to a standstill. Rommel was forced to retire.

A few days later the Eighth Army, with the remaining units of the magnificent New Zealand division, relieved Tobruk.

Rommel gathered his army together and fell back three hundred miles to his original Agheila Line. The Eighth Army, with weakened ranks, tried to pursue him through the quagmires caused by the winter rains, but their vehicles were bogged down and their extended columns slowed to a standstill. Although Rommel suffered a severe defeat, he saved his armies from destruction.

Then, with lightning speed, disaster overcame the Eighth Army. On January 21, 1942, Rommel pounced, long before the British thought that he could recover. With his mastery of desert tactics, he outflanked the scattered forces of the Eighth Army, whose hard-won gains were swept away once again.

The German-Italian armies pushed on and halted on the Gazala Line about thirty miles from Tobruk, and the Eighth Army tried once more to form a line to save Egypt.

Worse was to come. On May 26 Rommel attacked the British positions in great force. As the battle swayed backward and forward over the open desert, men were taken prisoner and escaped three or four times, and companies were split and lost their commanders and their bearings. In the end the Eighth Army retreated in poor order across the frontier into Egypt. They finally made a desperate but stubborn stand on the Alamein Line, a position which ran for thirty-five miles between the Qattara Depression and the sea. The invading army had reached a point only forty miles from Alexandria and just over a hundred miles from Cairo.

On June 21 Tobruk surrendered. Its new garrison was not accustomed to the unsparing attack of the Afrika Korps, and thirty-three thousand men and a valuable accumulation of stores were captured. This was a crushing defeat.

Rommel, who had lately been promoted to Field Marshal, paused to collect much-needed reinforcements and supplies. He had only twelve tanks on the active list and barely enough fuel even to keep them going.

On June 29, 1942, Mussolini flew to North Africa. He brought with him his most impressive uniforms and most majestic regalia. Every detail was prepared for his triumphal entry into Cairo and Alexandria. He deeply resented Rommel's successes, and Rommel in return heartily despised the failure of the Italian armies. In this hour of conquest the two leaders were not on speaking terms.

By July 20, as the Alamein Line still held, Mussolini returned to Rome, leaving his personal luggage behind so that it would be on the spot for the victorious moment.

15

The Malta Story

THE STORY OF the defense of the island of Malta is
one of the great epics of the war.

Malta has played an important part in Mediterranean affairs from the earliest seafaring days, when
the Phoenician merchants established their trade
routes. In the Middle Ages, when the Knights of
Malta held the island, the battlements of Valletta
towered over the Grand Harbor, where the galleons
of many nations anchored. In those days captains
were compelled to land bags of soil as a tax on each
cargo, to help fertilize the barren sandstone island.

The island came into British possession after the
Napoleonic Wars, and since then her fortunes have
been linked to those of the Empire. When the opening of the Suez Canal in 1869 cut out the long sea
trip around the Cape of Good Hope, Malta stood
directly on the great new trade route joining East
and West.

Malta has always been dependent on sea-borne

supplies, for the land is poor. Lacemaking is the only industry, and everything has to be imported to keep the population going.

After the French fleet was crippled in 1940, the Italian fleet dominated the Mediterranean, and Malta found herself with an enemy on her doorstep, very little protection, and a meager store of food.

The British Government had not forgotten the importance of the island base and had planned to send fighter squadrons and antiaircraft guns for her defense. But the demands nearer home were so pressing, the Battle of the Atlantic and the Battle of Britain were such a drain on war material, that there was little to spare for Malta.

In the autumn of 1940, when the desert battles flared up in North Africa, the total fighting force on the Maltese airfields consisted of five Swordfish, which had led a leisurely peacetime life towing targets for gunnery practice, four sea Gladiators, and one old Queen Bee. The Swordfish were too slow for modern warfare, but the Gladiators did very well. One was damaged at the outset, but the other three, operating under the affectionate labels, Faith, Hope, and Charity, and gently nursed by their ground crews, held off the fainthearted attacks of the Italian Air Force for some weeks.

The War Cabinet in London had to make a difficult decision. They were called on to send fighters overseas to Malta while Britain herself was being heavily blitzed; but if the war in the Western Desert was to be won the defense of Malta was vital.

So the build-up started. In the face of Italian resistance, aircraft were flown in, and ground staff and stores were landed by submarines. The passage of convoys, carrying both weapons for the troops and the bare necessities of life for the Maltese population, had become an urgent undertaking.

British losses mounted dangerously. At the time when fighter aircraft were a matter of life and death to Malta a grim tragedy occurred. Twelve Hurricanes and two Skuas were sent off from the aircraft carrier *Argus*. In order to avoid risk to the carrier they took off at their extreme range of four hundred and fifty miles. But they were caught in an unrelenting head wind which ate up their fuel, and only five aircraft had enough to make a landfall; the other nine were lost with their pilots.

Soon Malta-based submarines and aircraft, growing in strength, were constantly attacking Italian convoys carrying supplies to Rommel in North Africa. It became very costly for the Germans to supply the Afrika Korps, and Hitler decided that Malta must be crushed. Early in 1941 large forces of the Luftwaffe moved into Sicily, and the limp performance of the Italian Air Force was expanded to a full-scale attack.

Throughout 1941 the Battle of Malta raged with increasing fury, the British battering the North African convoys and the Germans and Italians pounding the island. The fine buildings were pierced with gaping holes; the dockyard was an array of twisted cranes and wrecked machines; the Grand Harbor was a graveyard of sunken ships. But above all the enemy went for the airfields.

The Maltese people suffered with the British, enduring the miseries of eighteen months' remorseless bombing with amazing calm. A chain of huge sandstone caves ran under Valletta, rather like catacombs. Here many Maltese lived, fairly safe, but hungry and cold, dirty and tired. They had been British for more than a hundred years, and they trusted the R.A.F. and the Navy to get them out of their plight. When the air raid sirens sounded, the women shook their fists at the German planes and went underground. In April 1941 the island was awarded the George Cross for national bravery.

The tragic and glorious story of the Malta convoys had begun. The Royal and Merchant navies, fighting with unflinching resolution to reach the beleaguered island, suffered appalling losses and were beaten back.

Early in 1942 Hitler again decided that the defenses must be blotted out and the island captured, so he gave orders to step up the air attack. It had seemed to the weary defenders that they had faced the limit, but much worse was in store.

Bombers came over by day and night in a vicious stream, but the gun crews stuck grimly to their posts. Unable to focus the worn and splintered sights, they held their fire until the aircraft were on top of them, then they let go in a united barrage. Between the raids they tended their wounded and their guns; but as the defenses weakened the attacking bombers flew lower and did more damage.

Willing teams worked among the sea of craters on the airfields. The Army joined the R.A.F. and the Maltese workmen, struggling valiantly to keep small airstrips in use. They leveled narrow ribbons of ground which were inevitably torn to pieces in the next raid, when they leveled them again. When the Luftwaffe destroyed the hangars, new ones were rigged up from the shreds of the old. The devotion of the ground staff never faltered, but April dawned with only six aircraft left in action.

New aircraft were desperately needed, and at last forty-seven longed-for Spitfires flew in. But before the aircraft could refuel the enemy blitzed the airfields, and by the next morning only seventeen were fit to fly. This was a crushing blow.

By the spring of 1942 the United States was at war, and her ships were fighting with the British to pierce the blockade. But it was months since a convoy had won through, and starvation stared Malta in the face. The stocks of ammunition and fuel were almost exhausted; but the dominating anxiety was what the troops and civilians were going to eat. Rations were down to a minimum — a piece of bread and jam for breakfast, bread with a slice of canned beef for lunch, and more bread for supper. As there was no fuel for anything but the aircraft and the men were too weak to walk far, they lived in shelters on the airfields. There were no stoves to cook on. One fighter pilot said later: "Compared to Malta, the Battle of Britain was a picnic."

At the end of May sixty-two more Spitfires flew in, and this time the ground staff was ready for them. A few minutes after the aircraft landed, when the enemy roared over and shot up the airfields, the Spitfires had already refueled and were back in the air, ready to take on the attacking bombers. It was a triumph of organization.

In mid-June two convoys were assembled for the relief of Malta. Eleven merchant ships, with cruiser and destroyer escort under the command of Admiral Vian of *Altmark* fame, sailed from Alexandria on June 11. Two of the freighters were damaged on the first day but the rest sailed on. In "Bomb Alley," near Sicily, the enemy attacked with every means in their power, and two more freighters were lost. Shielding the rest with smoke screens, Admiral Vian fought off the concentrated fury of the Luftwaffe and large forces of the Italian fleet for four days, until on July 16 he was forced to return to Alexandria with the seven remaining freighters. If it had been humanly possible to fight the cargoes through he was the man to have done it. It was an amazing feat to bring back so many ships from the jaws of death — but it did not relieve Malta.

The other Allied convoy of six merchant ships left Gibraltar on June 11 too; but this stood a better chance, as it was protected by a stronger escort, including a battleship, two aircraft carriers, cruisers, and destroyers. In the violence of the battle that followed, all but two freighters were lost. In the early hours of June 16, as the two heroic survivors crept into the Grand Harbor, crowds gathered on the ruined ramparts, ignoring the air raid sirens to pay their awed and respectful tribute. Of the seventeen merchant ships that had set out from both ends of the Mediterranean only two had reached Malta.

In the following August the battered remnants of the next convoy were saluted with grateful reverence — eleven freighters had left Gibraltar and five had won through. The last to arrive was the American tanker *Ohio*. Almost disabled and an easy target for the attacking Junkers, her captain and crew had stubbornly refused to abandon ship. The fuel she carried was highly inflammable, and every second under bombardment was intensely dangerous; but they calculated the risk and brought her in.

The indomitable perseverance and courage of the men who sailed and fought in the Malta convoys is beyond belief. Every mile of the passage was a battle against overwhelming odds.

In the autumn of 1942 Malta's long ordeal drew to a triumphant close. The island had been given a new lease on life by the incoming convoys — small as they were — and her aircraft were hitting out at Rommel's supply lines and at the Luftwaffe. As the losses mounted the German pilots finally lost heart. The battle had been won.

16

Japan Strikes

BY DECEMBER 1941 Japan was ready to go to war. She planned to conquer the Far East by treachery and force and establish her new empire.

Since 1939 many Japanese dreams had come true. Hitler had served his ally well. Holland had been defeated and could no longer protect the Dutch East Indies. Britain was sorely pressed, her resources strained to the uttermost, and she had little left for the Pacific.

The United States alone held the power to hinder Japanese ambition. Her Pacific fleet stood strongly in the path of aggression. So the Japanese Imperial Command planned the infamous attack on Pearl Harbor to wipe it out by foul means. They hoped that, with her fleet in ruins, the United States would be too shaken to go to war and that Britain would be too fully occupied on other fronts.

These hopes soon died. On December 8, the day after Pearl Harbor, Congress declared that a "state of war has existed between the United States and the Empire of Japan." Almost simultaneously Great Britain and the Commonwealth also declared war on Japan.

On the morning of December 11 Germany and Italy declared war on the United States. Later that day, the U. S. Congress recognized a state of war existed "between the United States and Germany and the United States and Italy."

Japan was a highly industrial modern state, the only one in the Far East. A small country with a growing population, she was forced to buy from other countries essential supplies like rice (the staple diet of the people), tin, rubber, and oil. She wanted to expand and to be independent.

In 1905 Japan had gained a decisive victory in the Russo-Japanese War. It was the first time that Europeans had been defeated by an Asiatic nation, and it gave Japan very big ideas. She was also on the winning side in the First World War — without too much sacrifice — so war appeared a profitable concern.

China lay near at hand, with a vast store of undeveloped wealth and a backward peasant population. Since 1912, when the last Chinese Emperor was dethroned, she had been a republic. Torn by rival political parties and swept from time to time by floods and famine, China was no match for her efficient neighbor. For years Japan had been worming her way into Chinese territory, particularly Manchuria, the province nearest to Japan; and since

1937 the two countries had been at open though undeclared war, with China steadily losing ground.

Now Japan looked farther afield, to the rubber and tin in British Malaya, to the oil and fine spices in the Dutch East Indies of Java and Sumatra, and even as far as the fabulous treasures of India.

The Japanese Emperor Hirohito, "Revered Son of Heaven," was worshiped by his people. He lived in a splendid palace, the "Temple of Heaven," in Tokyo and often appeared mounted on a noble white horse. He was considered a divine being, enjoying devout homage but very little actual power.

The country had been governed since 1937 by General Tojo, a warlike military leader, who had modeled his powerful army on Nazi lines.

By century-old tradition the Japanese people choose death rather than defeat. They commit hara-kiri (suicide) to escape disgrace, or as a token of grief. In feudal times, when a noble lord died, his retainers killed themselves as a sign of respect. By long training the Japanese have come to accept sudden death as a matter of course. They are taught, too, that it is disgraceful to show their feelings — boys are brought up to endure intense agony without flinching. When it came to war this readiness to die and disregard for suffering made the Japanese a very formidable foe. With a strong fleet of aircraft carriers and a sternly disciplined army specially trained for jungle fighting, Japan was completely prepared to fight an all-out land, sea, and air war.

For some time America had been acutely anxious about Japanese intentions in the Pacific. During 1941 discussions had been going on between the governments of the two countries, with the United States striving desperately to avert war. The Japanese envoy was actually in Washington at the time of Pearl Harbor, undoubtedly sent there to disguise Japanese plans.

The United States had built up a system of defense with a chain of island bases like stepping-stones across the Pacific and an air fleet in the Philippine Islands. The British held the fortified outposts of Hong Kong and Singapore and kept a few troops in Malaya.

The backbone of the Japanese striking forces was their aircraft carrier fleet under Admiral Nagumo. He commanded ten fast modern carriers, each with about seventy-five aircraft. By spreading out his fleet he was able to launch simultaneously attacks on targets thousands of miles apart.

Within a few hours of the disaster at Pearl Harbor, from their floating bases Japanese bombers attacked American positions on Wake Island, Midway Island, and Guam, and wiped out the American Air Force in the Philippines. They then turned to British targets, bombing Hong Kong and Singapore and landing troops in Malaya. The map (page 134) shows the wide range of Japanese destruction.

The defense of Wake Island by a tiny garrison of under four hundred men of the Navy and Marines is one of the most valiant epics of the Pacific War.

The garrison at Wake had just heard of the attack on Pearl Harbor when the first assault hit them.

A Marine fighter squadron of twelve planes, under the command of Major Paul Putnam, had flown in a few days before. Most of the planes and many of the island guns were put out of action in the first attack, but the men made miraculous repairs. The bombing went on, and three days later the Japanese attempted a landing.

The defenders on Wake Island held their fire until they could hit the ships at point-blank range, sinking a cruiser, two destroyers, and a gunboat. The remainder of the landing force retired at high speed.

Then Japanese bombers pounded the island mercilessly. The garrison knew that they were being softened up for the next landing. Reconnaissance planes came over to pinpoint the gun positions for the bombers, so the gun crews on the island manned them by day and spent exhausting nights moving them to new sites.

After ten days of battering the next landing came in force. The garrison fought furiously. In hand-to-hand fighting on the beaches the Marines held off the swarming invaders until they were overcome by superior power on land, sea, and in the air. It was said of Wake Island that it fell "with colors flying and guns shooting to the last." The garrison received a Unit Citation from the President for exceptional devotion to duty.

Meanwhile the British had suffered a heavy naval disaster. The *Prince of Wales,* the newest and most powerful British battleship, which had carried Winston Churchill to his first meeting with President Roosevelt, arrived in Singapore just before the attack on Pearl Harbor, accompanied by the battleship *Repulse.* When Japanese troops landed in Malaya, the two battleships, under the command of Admiral Phillips, steamed north with a destroyer escort to attack the landing force.

At this time no one realized the deadly strength and accuracy of the Japanese air attack. The British warships were sighted by enemy scouts, and the Japanese dive bombers closed in. They hammered the ships with low-flying attacks, and the torpedo-carrying bombers found their mark. Both battleships were hit amidships and sank in a few hours. With them the last chance of curbing Japanese sea power disappeared.

In northern Malaya the Japanese landings went on against fierce resistance from a small force of British, Australian, and Indian troops, who were outmatched from the beginning. They had very few aircraft and no tanks at all to put up against the Japanese armor. In a short time the Japanese were reinforced by units of the Imperial Guard, their crack regiment, while the British reinforcements who were rushed up from Singapore were raw troops who had only just landed in the country and had never seen a jungle.

The defending army made a fighting retreat south-ward through paddy fields and past the precious tin mines and well-tended rubber plantations into the Malayan jungle. They were constantly ambushed by Japanese units who landed behind their lines.

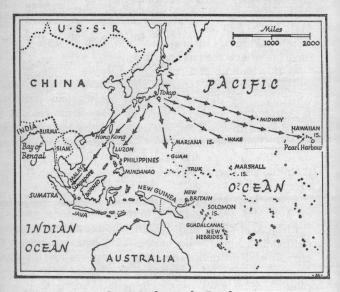

Japan strikes in the Pacific

They were short of food, bitten by leeches and mos-quitoes, and laid low with fever.

After seven weeks of continual Japanese pressure the retreating army was driven back to Singapore. This island base, at the tip of the Malayan peninsula, was considered impregnable — a symbol of British might; but its defense had always been planned to resist sea attack, and now the danger approached from the land. The great causeway which joined the island to the mainland was blown up by the Navy after the retreating army had crossed.

General Percival, commanding the forces in Singapore, prepared his tired troops for the coming battle. The Japanese massed in the jungle opposite the north shore of the island, where the thick forest growth hid their movements.

With a surprise attack, Japanese units gained a foothold on the island. In some sectors the defenders held their ground, but waves of fresh troops stormed in and forced them back, until they withdrew into Singapore city. Here the dispirited British troops were greeted by general panic. A flood of Asiatic refugees had poured into the city, and they were starving. The main reservoir had been hit, and the water supply was running out. They had been bombed for weeks and their dead were lying unburied in the streets.

General Percival knew that there was no hope of relief or evacuation, for orders from the Commander in Chief were clear — to fight it out to the end. After a week of siege the end came, for he decided that further defense was useless and surrendered with sixty thousand men. The flag of the Rising Sun was hoisted where the Union Jack had flown for a century. It was the worst defeat in British history.

17

The Battle of the Philippines

AMONG ALL THE ACTS of resistance to Japanese attacks, the heroic defense of the Bataan peninsula and of the little rocky island of Corregidor by American and Filipino troops stands as a shining example.

On December 8, 1941, the day after the Pearl Harbor attack, Japanese bombers blasted the Philippine airfields. After twenty-four hours of war the United States Far East Air Force was out of action. Then the Japanese landed in force. General MacArthur, who had just been made commander of all land forces in the Far East, placed his American and Filipino troops on a broad front across the island. They were beaten back by the attackers until they took up defensive positions on the peninsula of Bataan and the island of Corregidor.

Ninety thousand men with tanks, equipment, and some food withdrew to Bataan, a fine area for defense, twenty-five miles long and twelve miles wide. Rugged heights rise from dense jungle, clear streams spring from the volcanic rocks and jagged promontories jut into the sea, commanding the flat, swampy beaches between.

The Japanese attacked first from the land and then with sea-borne landings behind the American lines. Every assault was repelled in bitter fighting. The Japanese wedged themselves in clefts in the cliffs until they were blasted out with dynamite. Their losses were so heavy that General Homma, their Commander in Chief, sent out aircraft over the beaches to drop orders in sealed bamboo tubes, recalling the survivors.

Japanese aircraft also dropped leaflets to the defenders, telling them that their fight was hopeless. Some of the leaflets were lavishly illustrated with drawings of luscious food.

The Bataan garrison eked out their food as best they could. From the first they were on short rations, and as the weeks passed their situation grew desperate. They harvested the meager crops of rice, scoured the jungle for anything they could eat and finally slaughtered their horses and pack mules. By March the defending army was gaunt and shrunken with starvation and fever; but still they held on. They always hoped for relief, but the Allied navies dared not risk the ships.

General MacArthur set up his headquarters on the little tadpole-shaped island of Corregidor, lying off the tip of the Bataan peninsula. From there he directed the battle with skill and experience born of wide knowledge of the Far East. MacArthur had lived for years in the Philippines. He knew the conditions and he knew the Japanese. He was determined to share the dangers and privations of his men and to remain on Corregidor until the end of the siege.

In the Pentagon and the White House there was deep concern. General MacArthur's wisdom and leadership were too valuable to the Allied cause to be cast away. They could not afford to lose the man who might sway the course of the Pacific War. An order went out for him to leave the Philippines and proceed to Australia. He ignored it. In a personal command from President Roosevelt MacArthur's duty was made clear.

Secretly, by night, a submarine stole into a little bay on the rocky coast of Corregidor. As General MacArthur reluctantly went on board with his wife and young son he made the solemn promise which was to be remembered through the years: "I shall return."

The submarine threaded its perilous way through Japanese-guarded waters to Australia. There General MacArthur took over the command of the Allied Armed Land Forces in the Pacific.

General Wainwright assumed command in Corregidor and General King under him in Bataan.

By April twelve thousand men had died on Bataan, and the rest were too weak to man the defenses. Upheld only by their courage, they had almost ceased to be a fighting force. Then General Homma launched a massive attack and cracked the center of the slender line of defense. With his men driven into the jungle and scattered, his hospitals overflowing, and no chance of relief, General King saw that resistance was at an end. On April 9 he sadly sent out two convoys, bearing white flags, to General Homma.

The Battle of Bataan ended in gruesome tragedy. When the gallant army had surrendered, the men were lined up for the march to the prison camps. In the broiling sun, for sixty-five miles, they were driven like animals by their Japanese captors. They were denied food and water, and when they fell by the wayside they were clubbed and beaten back into the ranks. It became known as the "Death March" and is remembered as one of the most brutal of wartime atrocities.

The appalling horrors of the Japanese prison camps were just unfolding. As death, to the Japanese, is not important in the Western sense, they are careless of their own lives and utterly merciless to others. When they conquered a country they rounded up not only the defeated armies but the European civilians too. In the prison camps men and women were starved and tortured, driven out to work at the point of a bayonet, and flogged to death if they collapsed. The guards mixed savage brutality with gross neglect. Thousands of prisoners died.

On Corregidor General Wainwright organized his troops to fight on. Corregidor had strong fortifications, and a network of tunnels ran under the island. It had long been a fort protecting Manila, the capital of the Philippines.

By April the garrison had suffered months of bombing and lack of food. Now Homma moved his artillery to the tip of Bataan, and a ceaseless bombardment set in. The shelling was far more deadly than the bombing. The defenses were shattered, and nothing was left alive aboveground. Lumps of concrete and splintered rock lay in great ragged piles. Somehow the gunners kept a few of the coastal batteries in action. Casualties were heavy, but heroism was undimmed. Once a shell splinter cut the halyard of the American flag, and it began to fall from the tall flagpole. Captain Arthur Huff and three volunteers left their shelter during intense bombardment, caught the flag before it reached the ground, repaired the halyard, and raised it again. They were awarded Silver Stars.

When the Japanese finally attempted a landing they were amazed to find that a barrage of fire greeted them. But Homma sent reinforcements in, and General Wainwright decided that further resistance was suicidal. He told the President that "the limit of human endurance has long since been passed."

He lowered the Stars and Stripes, hoisted a white flag in its stead, and went into captivity with his men. The southern island of Mindanao fell a few days later, but it had taken the Japanese five months to subdue the Philippine Islands.

18

North African Victory

WHEN TOBRUK FELL in June 1942 Winston Churchill was in the United States. After six months of war
against Japan there were matters of grave conse-
quence to be discussed by the President of the
United States and the Prime Minister of Great Britain. They were working together in all things for a
single end.

Two top-secret decisions had to be made. The
first was the future of the devastating new weapon
now in the early stages of creation — the atom bomb.

The second, when and where the Anglo-American forces could make a landing in Europe.

For a year Russia had held out by a narrow margin against the monstrous might of Germany. The
Soviet armies were nearly spent, and the only way
to lessen the pressure was to make an attack which
would force Hitler's armies to fight on other fronts
as well.

The defeat in the desert deepened the gloom in

an already somber scene. In the Pacific one Japanese victory had led swiftly to another. The United States fleet lay in ruins, and the important British base of Singapore had been lost. In the Battle of the Atlantic the U-boats were creating havoc in American shipping lanes, and disaster still overshadowed the Malta convoys. Few gleams of success brightened the darkness of the Allied horizon.

Fortunately a resolute team was gathered in Washington in these critical June days. President Roosevelt and Mr. Churchill had with them General Marshall, Commander in Chief of the United States Army, General Sir Alan Brooke, Chief of the Imperial General Staff, and many expert advisers.

When the news of the British defeat in the Western Desert came through, General Marshall instantly diverted three hundred of America's brand-new Sherman tanks, eagerly awaited by his own army, into the breach. It was a magnificent gesture and, as it turned out, an excellent military decision.

How should the Grand Alliance set about liberating Europe? Hitler had ringed all the coasts with gun emplacements and airfields, and talked of "Fortress Europa." An Allied invasion of France at that date would have been doomed to failure. So it was decided that the only chance of a successful Anglo-American landing lay in North Africa. If the line at Alamein could be held and an Allied army established in Algeria, Rommel would be forced to split his forces.

So "Operation Torch" was planned for the autumn of 1942.

Armed with this resolution, Winston Churchill flew home from America, and before long he set out to see for himself the situation in Egypt. For safety's sake his route by air had been plotted on a wide curve, well away from Nazi bases. It would have been long, tedious, and hot touching down in tropical Africa to refuel. Then Churchill heard that a young American pilot, Captain Vanderkloot, had converted a Liberator bomber to fly farther, without refueling, than any other passenger plane. This suited Winston Churchill well. Sleeping in a converted bomb rack, he cut straight across Europe and reached Cairo in two days, and from then on he made many long trips through hostile skies with Captain Vanderkloot.

Cairo had been thrown into a state of panic at the near approach of the German armies. The smoke from the bonfires of secret and semisecret papers had hung over the city for days. People suddenly found themselves very near the front line, and they were unprepared.

On August 3 Churchill arrived and immediately visited the Alamein positions. A spirit of uncertainty reigned, for it was obvious that something drastic had to be done; yet no one knew what was going to happen next.

After careful consideration, General Sir Harold Alexander was appointed Commander in Chief,

Middle East, to succeed General Auchinleck. Under him was needed a commander in the field, and the finest choice appeared to be General Gott, who was nicknamed "Strafer" Gott with reason. He was given the vital task of rallying and commanding the Eighth Army for the coming offensive; but on his way to take up the new appointment he was shot down by a German gunner and killed, leaving a gap that could be filled only be a great general.

General Bernard Montgomery was taken away from his job in the Torch expedition and given command of the Eighth Army. From the moment that "Alex" and "Monty," as they soon came to be called, took over the command of the Middle East forces, the outlook changed. Confidence replaced fear, and determination drove away doubt.

Alex was a born leader, with a calm, almost gay contempt for danger, and men had followed him without question. He had shown absolute steadfastness on the beaches of Dunkirk and in the Burma jungle.

Monty was a different kind of soldier. He was a rigid disciplinarian and did not spare himself or anyone else. He had dedicated his life to his job and had worked on military strategy for years. He inspired faith from the day he arrived in the desert by moving from unit to unit, talking to officers and men, getting to know them all. Monty lived in his famous caravan captured from the Italians, half office and half bedroom, near the front line. One of the few adornments in his office was a large portrait of Rommel.

On the second day of his command in the Western Desert, Monty gathered his officers together and spoke to them: "The defense of Egypt lies here at Alamein and on Ruweisat Ridge. If you are attacked there will be no retreat. If we cannot stay here alive, then we will stay here dead. These orders have already gone out." It was a clear command; there was no place in the Eighth Army for anyone who questioned it or was not prepared to carry it out.

Winston Churchill flew on from Cairo to Moscow in the Liberator with Captain Vanderkloot, to see Stalin. The two leaders had never met face to face, and it was important that Stalin should be told of the secret plans for the invasion of French North Africa.

In Egypt preparations went on for the great battle against Rommel. New tanks rolled in, Grants and Shermans from America and Churchills from Britain, and tank-recovery carriers and long-range anti-tank guns. General Montgomery worked out his desert strategy and trained his men, for every soldier had to be "desert-worthy."

Aircraft were accumulated behind the front in Egypt, and in Malta the airfields were restocked. The island had survived her ordeal and was ready to take part in the next battle.

Meanwhile in Washington and London preparaations for the North Africa landing were speeding up. American and British troops would land at Casablanca on the coast of Morocco, at Algiers and Oran in Algeria. They would advance eastward to link up with Montgomery's Eighth Army advancing from Alamein. Thus Rommel's armies would be encircled and destroyed. It was a giant operation, the first test of the Grand Alliance, and the planners lived through nerve-racking days.

A huge concentration of ships and landing barges had to be assembled secretly at Gibraltar from American and British ports. If General Franco had taken Spain to war on the side of the Axis, the enterprise would have been impossible. His guns would have held the invasion fleet at point-blank range. Fortunately for the Allies he disappointed his Axis friends, who had put him in power, and kept his country neutral.

General Dwight D. Eisenhower had come from America as Commander in Chief of the Allied armies in French North Africa. "Ike" was to prove one of the greatest figures of the war, and later to become the thirty-fourth president of the United States. He was a fine team leader, proud to be American, yet seeing clearly the point of view of other nations. His tact and wisdom never failed, and under his command the Allied armies united into one vast force, confident of their leader.

General Mark Clark arrived in Britain as his Deputy Commander in Chief. He was a man of resource and daring, a tough disciplinarian, respected but also greatly loved by his men. Mark Clark was the youngest man in the Army's history to gain the three stars of a lieutenant general.

Before the landing he was chosen to lead a secret mission to North Africa to prepare the loyal French for the invasion. By plane, submarine, and rubber dinghy the party crept in by night, kept their rendezvous and barely escaped with their lives twenty-four hours later.

General James H. Doolittle commanded the American air forces, and General George S. Patton the Army corps that would make the attack on Casablanca, going directly by ship from the United States. "Blood and Guts" Patton was the foremost American expert on tank warfare, and his dash and skill in leading his armored forces were to grow into a legend for his allies and nightmare for his enemies.

While the commanders of "Operation Torch" prayed for calm seas and cloudy skies to conceal the landing force from the Luftwaffe, the War Cabinet in London anxiously awaited news from Alamein. The word "Zip," signaled by General Alexander to Churchill, was to announce the opening of the battle.

On September 30, 1942, Rommel attacked. He tried to swing south, beyond the Eighth Army defenses, and then wheel up to their rear, bottling up large forces. It was the old game, and Montgomery had foreseen this precise move. He had placed his best troops exactly where Rommel had hoped to find a weakness. The Afrika Korps had met its match at last, both in leadership and in armor. After three days of heavy fighting, without cracking the Alamein defense, Rommel had to withdraw. Montgomery did not fling his army into the pursuit; he was not yet ready for the supreme blow.

British, Australian, New Zealand, South African, Polish, Greek, and Free French troops were all enrolled in the Eighth Army. After the repulse of the German-Italian armies their morale was high. They were convinced that Monty would not fail. The whole Alamein front was tense with expectation, and each man knew his job.

The attack was due at full moon, two weeks before "Torch." On October 23 "Zip" was signaled to Britain.

General Montgomery opened the battle with a tremendous barrage from a thousand guns and a blanket of air bombardment. Then deep mine fields had to be cleared by the engineers before the tanks could move forward.

Rommel had been ill for some time, and when the attack opened he was in the hospital in Germany. He got out of bed and returned to the front. He had other troubles, too, for his supply lines had been under constant attack, and half the ships never reached North Africa. He was very short of fuel — the more tankers the Germans sent, the more the Allies sank.

Nevertheless, the German defense was stubborn, and the battle raged around the Alamein positions for ten days, with both sides attacking and counterattacking in force. The Eighth Army strove for a breakthrough with sharp, probing attacks. For the first time they ran a good tank-recovery service, and every tank was needed.

At last, on November 4, a wedge was driven into the German lines; the front was pierced, and the next day Rommel's armies were in retreat. Then the long pursuit set in. Once more Rommel retired to his Agheila position with the Eighth Army on his heels.

On November 8 the Allied armies invaded French

The Afrika Korps trapped in Tunis

North Africa. Self-propelled barges carried the troops to the beaches, and the landing went according to plan. The secret of Torch had been well kept, for German and Italian spies had merely reported a large-scale convoy from Gibraltar to Malta. American troops took the lead, for it was hoped that Frenchmen would not resist American invaders as fiercely as British. The United States did not share in the blame for the sinking of the French fleet in 1940, as she had been neutral at the time. There was, in fact, no great opposition except in the main ports, where the invaders had to face point-blank fire, and the casualties were very heavy.

Once the troops were ashore, the Allied command had hoped to enlist a French leader, General Giraud, to give friendly aid and rally Frenchmen against the Vichy Government. Unfortunately Giraud did not come up to expectations.

It happened that Admiral Darlan, Commander in Chief of the French fleet under Vichy, was in Algiers visiting his son, who was ill. He offered to work for the Allies and to take control of the local people, preventing bloodshed. It was a difficult decision for General Eisenhower to make. If he did not use Admiral Darlan, thousands of Frenchmen, Americans, and British would be killed in fruitless fighting. But on the other hand it seemed wrong to deal with a servant of the detested Vichy regime. Darlan had first betrayed France and was now betraying Vichy. In the end Eisenhower decided to use him as a stopgap.

When Hitler heard of the North African landings he immediately occupied the southern part of
France. This was the territory that, by the terms of
the Armistice, he had promised to leave under
French control. Marshal Pétain, head of the Vichy
Government, was very old and powerless to resist,
and Laval, his second-in-command, was pro-Nazi
anyway. The remains of the French fleet lay in
Toulon Harbor, and the German Army was sweeping down toward the Mediterranean to capture it.
Darlan ordered the fleet to North Africa, but the
admiral in command would not put to sea. Then,
just before the Germans entered Toulon, patriotic
French naval officers scuttled every ship. Each commander stayed on the bridge of his ship until it
sank, and many died there. Seventy-three ships
foundered that day. Thus the last of the French
fleet evaded capture, once again by tragic means.

A month later Darlan was shot down in the street
in Algiers by a young Frenchman who ardently
wished to rid his country of an evil influence.

In January 1943 the Eighth Army captured Tripoli
and pressed back the German-Italian armies to the
Tunisian border. From the west General Eisenhower was grouping his forces for an all-out attack.

On April 22 seven months after General Montgomery had attacked at Alamein, the Allies began
to close in on Rommel's encircled armies from both
sides, and the British fleet patrolled the Tunisian
coast to prevent an Axis Dunkirk.

On May 12 the Allied armies joined hands. Rommel himself had escaped by air, but the rest of the trapped Afrika Korps had to surrender. A quarter of a million troops laid down their arms; the Afrika Korps ceased to exist, and the enemy was completely cleared from North Africa. It was a tremendous triumph.

19

Stalingrad Defeats Hitler

MEANWHILE, THE BATTLES between the two titanic armies of Germany and Russia raged on. When the struggle first broke out, long before the desert victory, Britain had to consider how she could help Russia.

There were three ways: first, by attacking the German and Italian forces in the Mediterranean and holding down their troops; second, by bombing Germany; third, by sending supplies which Russia needed.

The sending of supplies presented a serious transport problem. They could go by ship around the Cape of Good Hope and up the Persian Gulf, and from there by truck or single-track railroad across Persia or Iraq, a trip of about ten thousand miles; or they could be shipped to Murmansk or Archangel in northern Russia, a perilous trip around the German-occupied coast of Norway and into the stormy Arctic Circle.

The famous Murmansk convoys started in August 1941. In theory the supplies were to be taken in Russian ships, but in practice the Russians could only provide enough to carry about a quarter of the goods. The rest were carried in British and American vessels.

The convoys sailed without much opposition until the following March, when the Germans started to attack in force with Norway-based aircraft and submarines.

It was a major sacrifice to take escort ships for these Arctic convoys off the Atlantic routes, where the toll of shipping losses was rising steadily; but it was vitally important to prevent a Russian collapse.

The scale of the German attack mounted. The Arctic conditions, the danger from ice floes, and the Nazi bombardment made the Murmansk convoys unique in their hardship.

In June 1942 a convoy of thirty-four merchant ships set out from Iceland, with an escort of destroyers, antiaircraft, and rescue ships, with cruisers standing by. The convoy was attacked, and twenty-three merchant ships were lost with their crews, who were killed outright or died of exposure in the icy waters. Only eleven ships straggled into Murmansk Harbor at the end of the melancholy voyage.

The escorts were strengthened, and the ships fought through. In the September convoy, of the thirty-nine cargo ships that started, twelve were lost.

In the spring of 1942 Hitler had renewed his attack on Russia. He had been cheated of victory the year before, but with the fine spring weather his dreams of glory revived.

The Russians had not been idle during the winter. Long before the war they had built armament factories in the Ural Mountains, far from the range of the German bombers and now untouched by the invasion. Tanks and guns were laboriously transported hundreds of miles on the single-track railroads to supply the long front. Fresh reserves were brought in from the abundant store of Russian man power to reinforce the Red Army.

Hitler refused to believe reports of Soviet strength or of Soviet determination. He made his main attack in the south, toward the oil fields of the Caucasus. Baku, the richest of them all, was his ultimate goal.

General Kleist, with a Panzer army of fifteen divisions, penetrated the Russian lines and pushed ahead for several hundred miles. But each oil field that they captured had been destroyed by the retreating Red Army, and not a single drop of oil reached the Nazi war machines.

Sevastopol was captured, together with the Russian Black Sea fleet, but these limited triumphs took the German armies all summer, instead of being the swift, decisive punch that Hitler had planned.

On the flank of the German advance stood the city of Stalingrad. Partly because of its name and partly because of its factories, Stalingrad was highly important to both sides. Hitler staked everything on its capture. He sent the Sixth Army under General von Paulus to storm the city, together with strong forces of the Luftwaffe.

Then followed one of the deadliest battles of the war. The Red Army defended Stalingrad with passionate fury, fighting every yard of the way, both sides suffering terrible losses.

Von Paulus drove his weary troops into the outskirts, fighting from factory to factory and house to house. His supply line was thin and winter was coming on, but Hitler would not hear of withdrawal; he rejected all warnings.

So the army under General von Paulus continued to forge its way into the ruins of the city, and the general himself was promoted to Field Marshal to spur him on to greater efforts. It was in vain, for on November 19 the Red Army launched a carefully prepared counterattack, cut the enemy supply lines, and trapped the German Sixth Army.

Hitler sent orders for Field Marshal von Paulus to hold out until he was relieved, and for seven desperate weeks the Germans dug in among the ruins of Stalingrad and beat off the Russian attacks. The troops grew short of food, ammunition, and medical supplies; they were bitterly cold, and many of them were dying of typhus. Finally, on January 31, 1943, Field Marshal von Paulus and ninety thousand men, the only survivors of the great army, surrendered.

The siege of Stalingrad marked the turning point of the war. From then on, Hitler never won another victory.

20

The Tide Turns Against Japan

AFTER THE FALL of Singapore the way was clear for the Japanese conquest of the Dutch East Indies, the lovely islands of Sumatra, Java, Timor, and Bali, which had been under Dutch rule for three and a half centuries.

Plans were laid for obstinate Allied resistance. General Wavell, who had earlier whipped the Italians in North Africa, took charge of the Dutch, Australian and British forces in Java, and a small fleet of Allied ships under the brave command of the Dutch Admiral Helfrich sailed against the massive enemy fleet. But the storm of Japanese conquest swept on. Almost all the Allied ships, including the *Exeter* of River Plate fame, were sunk. On March 8 Java surrendered, and as there was no navy left to evacuate the troops, they passed into the nightmare of Japanese prison camps.

By the spring of 1942 the Japanese had gained one victory after another without losing a single aircraft carrier and with their army almost intact. But while they prepared for even greater triumphs, American commanders were neither defeatist nor idle. In Washington Admiral Ernest J. King, Commander in Chief of the Navy, and General Henry ("Hap") Arnold, head of the Army Air Force, discussed how they could carry the war to Japan. The problems were immense. Carrier-based aircraft did not have the flying range to bomb Japan from a point where the carriers could launch them. The fate of the *Repulse* and the *Prince of Wales* was in everyone's mind. They called in Colonel Jimmy Doolittle, one of the most experienced and daring pilots in the Air Force, to help.

They worked out a fabulous plan to train pilots to fly medium bombers from a flight deck, ship them as near Japan as they dared, and then send them off to raid Tokyo, trusting that they would be able to fly on and land on friendly airfields in China.

The training under Colonel Doolittle began. A strip on Eglin Field in Florida was measured out, and the pilots practiced taking off in this small area. They realized that the strip represented the flight deck of an aircraft carrier, but they did not know where the carrier was going to take them. The mission was so dangerous that each of the men who flew in or serviced the sixteen aircraft was a volunteer. There were seventy officers and a hundred and thirty enlisted men.

Admiral Nimitz, Commander in Chief at Pearl

Harbor, chose Admiral Halsey's task force to launch the raid. In great secrecy the bombers were loaded onto the carrier *Hornet.* She sailed with Admiral Halsey in his flagship, the carrier *Enterprise,* and a cruiser and destroyer escort. When they were well out at sea the target was announced, final details were fixed and the pilots briefed. The enthusiasm was tremendous.

Admiral Halsey hoped to take the *Hornet* to within five hundred miles of Tokyo. The pilots would then have another thousand miles before they could land in China. It was calculated that this was the safety limit of their flying range.

When the force was seven hundred miles from Japan it was sighted by a Japanese ship. The situation was critical. The Japanese might attack at any moment. The *Hornet* was defenseless, with the bombers spread on her flight deck, and the distance was beyond the safety limit. Also, they had planned a night raid and now it was daylight.

However, Jimmy Doolittle decided to strike. Six hundred and sixty-eight miles from Tokyo he led his squadrons off. None of the pilots had ever taken off from a carrier before, but the training held good and they all got safely away.

At noon on April 18, 1942, war came to the Japanese people. The raiding force did their work well. The surprise was complete. They found their targets, and not a single plane was lost over Tokyo.

Then came the flight to an unknown landing.

The Chinese thought that the American bombers were enemy planes and gave them no help on the airfields. They made crash landings or bailed out as best they could. One plane came down in the sea, and the crew was captured by the Japanese. Some of the men were killed or wounded, but of the eighty fliers who set out, Colonel Doolittle and seventy other men survived.

The courage of the men who flew to Tokyo was rewarded. The raid raised morale in America and among her allies in the darkest days of the war. Hopes rose, and people suddenly felt that they were a match for the Japanese. And in Japan valuable fighter squadrons were tied down to guard against another attack.

In this same month the Americans made their first naval challenge. Admiral Nimitz, commanding the United States Pacific fleet from Pearl Harbor, got reports of a Japanese naval striking force heading south toward Australia. If the Japanese could capture the islands near New Guinea, their ships and aircraft could range freely over the Coral Sea to the coast of Australia. Under the shadow of Japanese air power Australia would be cut off from her Allies and forced out of the war.

Admiral Nimitz gathered together in the Coral Sea all available Allied warships. By great good fortune the aircraft carriers had been at sea during the raid on Pearl Harbor, so they had escaped damage. Two of them under the command of Admiral

Fletcher, the *Yorktown* and the *Lexington,* were within call. The other two, the *Enterprise* and the *Hornet,* had launched the Doolittle raid over Japan and were thousands of miles away.

On May 8 the Japanese attacked. It was the first great aircraft carrier battle. Not a single shot was fired by the warships — the aircraft struck the blows. Though separated by miles of ocean, the opposing forces were locked in combat.

The carriers sent off their own bombers and zig-zagged to escape destruction from enemy bombs and torpedoes. Planes flew in and refueled under a barrage of fire. Losses on both sides were heavy in aircraft and men. The *Yorktown* and *Lexington* were both hit, and the Japanese carrier *Shoko* was sunk. The smoke over the American carriers was so dense that Japanese pilots reported that both vessels were at the bottom of the Coral Sea.

After the battle the crew fought to quench the fires on the *Yorktown* and got them under control. She was badly damaged but kept going under her own steam. The *Lexington* was listing, and fires were burning below deck. The ship's company, under the command of Captain Sherman, fought the blaze, and for a time it seemed as if the "Lady Lex" would live to fight again. Suddenly a deafening explosion rocked the carrier. Fire burst from below deck, and a sheet of flame covered the bomb storage compartment. Other explosions followed, and Captain Sherman had to order the crew to

abandon ship. The most beloved ship in the United
States Navy was doomed. The men leaped from the
flight deck while the wounded were lowered, calmly and in perfect order, to the boats.

The Japanese fleet retired, having met with their
first reverse. The Allied fleet suffered heavy losses,
but they had done what they set out to do: the
Coral Sea was saved.

An even greater battle loomed ahead, for Midway
Island, in the mid-Pacific, was still in American
hands. It is a barren, rocky dot about six miles
across; but it stood as a sentry guarding the Hawaiian Islands with their naval base of Pearl Harbor. If the Japanese took Midway, they could command the air and sea around Pearl Harbor.

Admiral Yamamoto, Commander in Chief of the
Japanese Navy, sailed out to battle in his super-
battleship *Yamato*. His plans were very simple —
first to capture Midway Island and then to wipe
out the United States fleet when it came to the
rescue.

Midway was primed for the battle. Her airfields
were packed with aircraft and her garrison of Marines reinforced. The fleet prepared to defend the
island, but the commanders knew they were outnumbered. They had no battleships and only three
carriers. The *Enterprise* and the *Hornet,* under Admiral Spruance, were back from the Tokyo raid, and
the *Yorktown* had limped in after the Battle of the

Coral Sea. By a stupendous effort, the Pearl Harbor navy yard had gotten her back on the active list in two days.

The Japanese had brought out four fast carriers — the flagship *Akagi* carrying Admiral Nagumo, the *Kaga* (meaning "increased joy"), the *Soryu,* and the *Hiryu* — with strong battleship escort. These very carriers had sent off the bombers to Pearl Harbor six months before.

On June 4 Midway got warning of bombers on the horizon. The raid was severe and the island badly damaged, but the gunners took a heavy toll of Japanese planes, and they saved the airfields. None of their own aircraft was caught on the ground.

Admiral Yamamoto decided that another strike would finish off Midway, so he ordered all his planes back to their carriers to refuel and fill up their bomb racks.

Then Admiral Spruance sent off from the *Enterprise* and *Hornet* every combat plane that he could command. Wildcat fighters, Devastator torpedo planes, and Dauntless dive bombers soared away until the hangars were bare. Spruance timed the arrival of his bombers over the Japanese carriers when their flight decks would be crammed with aircraft. For once the Japanese pilots found themselves helpless — at the receiving end of the bomb run.

It was a wonderfully clear day, with high fluffy

clouds. When the American pilots had gained height they could see their targets fifty miles away over the calm sea.

Lieutenant Commanders Waldron, Lindsey, and Massey led in with their squadrons of torpedo bombers. They had no fighter cover, and were too slow to escape the antiaircraft fire. They pressed home their low-level attack, holding their course, never swerving from almost certain death. Their courage was boundless and their sacrifice infinite; out of forty-one bombers only six returned. Without them the battle could never have been won, for they kept the Japanese aircraft pinned to the flight decks until the dive bombers came.

Led by Lieutenant Commander McClusky from the *Enterprise* and Lieutenant Commander Leslie from the *Hornet*, the Dauntless dive bombers followed up and raked Yamamoto's carriers with fire. The newly fueled aircraft were packed like sardines on the flight decks. When the bombs fell among them they burst into a sea of flame. Burning oil spurted from their tanks, and the loaded bombs went up in a salvo of explosions. The carriers turned into raging infernos.

In the Battle of Midway the Japanese lost four of their fastest aircraft carriers, two hundred and fifty aircraft, and, most serious of all, their best air crews. Their crack pilots, who had been so carefully trained, were dead and could not be replaced.

The American carrier *Yorktown* had been sunk

and many fine young pilots killed, but the might of
Japan was shaken. Through the skill and courage
of the men who fought at Midway, a corner on the
road to victory had been turned. The Japanese
spearhead had been blunted by the navy they had
thought was finished.

21

In the Shadow of the Swastika

Pᴇᴏᴘʟᴇ ᴡʜᴏ ʟɪᴠᴇ in a free country like the United States can speak and act and worship openly, without fear of persecution. Hitler's reign was one of tyranny and terror. It is important to grasp what was happening in Germany under the Nazi regime, where freedom had died and fear ruled.

Hitler had gained an almost magic power over the German people. They followed him with superstitious faith, the "Man of Destiny," who had been sent to make Germany great once more.

From the first day in kindergarten children came under Nazi pressure. They were never allowed to decide anything for themselves; words were put into their mouths and thoughts into their minds. Teachers who did not support the Nazi Party lost their jobs. Children said Nazi prayers, read Nazi lesson books, and listened to Nazi broadcasts. They could not judge whether Hitler's ways were good or bad, because they had never known anything else.

As they grew older the boys and girls were enrolled in the Hitler *Jugend* (Hitler Youth). It took up most of their spare time. They were given work to do for the Party, and Nazi training was tied up with games and community singing, so that it was good fun.

Unconsciously the children learned intolerance and hate. They grew up despising the weak and worshiping Hitler. By the time they were old enough to think things out, they had either lost all sense of right and wrong or were governed only by fear.

When Hitler was building up the strength of the Nazi Party he formed an armed guard who attended him regularly — the SA troops, the jack-booted "Brownshirts." They were professional thugs, whose main duty was to protect Nazi meetings and break up others. Later he formed a more exclusive corps of Nazi Guards, the SS.

When he became dictator, Hitler expanded the SS and founded the *Gestapo* (secret police). They grew into a tremendous force under the command of Heinrich Himmler, whose name soon became an emblem of brutality. The Gestapo was the whip Hitler used to discipline the German people. The reign of terror had started.

Jews were the main victims of Hitler's persecution. When he first came to power he was content to seize their goods and drive them out of the country. Later, as a conquering hero, he stopped caring what other nations thought and set up apparatus for mass murder.

Hitler had always laid the blame on the German Jews for the country's misfortunes, making them the scapegoats for the German defeat in 1918 and for her poverty later. This hatred of Jews was the cornerstone of Hitler's policy, and was expressed in *Mein Kampf* when he swore to "exterminate them," to wipe them out by every means in his power, so that Germany would prosper.

He allowed no whisper of criticism against the Nazi regime. Huge concentration camps were opened to imprison Jews and anyone who spoke openly. There was no question of trial or justice, no chance to prove innocence or guilt. The Gestapo hounded down Jews and "political offenders" and carried them off. Those who could flee the country did so, but many others were herded into sealed vans or railroad trucks and flung into the camps. There they lived or died in conditions of utter misery, fear, and squalor.

The punishment varied. Men and women slaved in quarries or at other hard labor until they collapsed from starvation or illness. The daily ration was turnip and potato soup and a little black bread. The other penalty was death. Millions of blameless, intelligent Jews were stripped of their clothes and possessions and marched into gas chambers. They died for no other crime than belonging to the Jewish race in the reign of Adolf Hitler.

As the Nazis overran the neighboring countries new concentration camps sprang up to satisfy Hitler's blood lust. Everyone within the reach of the Gestapo lived in the shadow of death. Nothing can wipe from the pages of German history the dark stain left by the names of Belsen, Buchenwald, Dachau, Mauthausen, Auschwitz, and many other camps. Auschwitz was the most dreaded of all, and few prisoners came out of it alive. The concentration camps were staffed by SS troops who, blinded by their faith in the Führer, had no room for pity.

Yet it must not be forgotten that there were always individual Germans who risked everything because of their belief in humanity, to protect the persecuted. They sheltered the hunted Jews and political fugitives and helped them to escape, although their own lives were at stake.

In 1939 the younger Germans had been keen to go to war. They had been taught to believe that they were the rightful masters of Europe, heroes of the New Order. They were ardent in their desire to fight for their Führer. The older generation were nervous and worried. They remembered the suffering of the First World War, and they did not want to go through it again.

However, when the Nazis conquered one country after another, enthusiasm swept through Germany. It became a popular war, and each easy triumph was greeted with relief and rejoicing. When Paris fell, Hitler staged a victory parade in Berlin; it seemed then that the fighting would soon be over, with very little German sacrifice. For the German people the summer of 1940 was the greatest moment of the war. No one supposed that Britain would hold out much longer against the overwhelming Nazi might. The Führer was leading them on to swift victory, and Germany was invincible.

Propaganda was one of Hitler's favorite weapons. By a steady stream of lies, the German people were brought into line with Nazi plans. They were forbidden to tune in to foreign broadcasts lest they should hear the truth. The penalties for disobedience were severe: the Gestapo had spies everywhere, and the concentration camps were waiting.

In Goebbels, Minister of Propaganda, Hitler found one of his most sinister and devoted followers — the able mouthpiece of the Nazi machine.

During the winter of 1940, though Britain had not surrendered, lurid descriptions of the blitz filled the press, and the German radio gloated over the devastation. Field Marshal Göring had said of the bombing: "This is the final act of the war."

He had also said in the summer: "No British bomb shall ever touch a German city." But by this time a few British bombers were, in fact, reaching Germany, and the prospects of a speedy Nazi victory were not quite as rosy as they had been six months before.

Nevertheless, faith in Hitler did not falter. In face of facts, he always managed to persuade the German people that he was blessed with divine power. When defeat finally loomed large, he kept up morale with the "miracle weapons," which he was holding "until the time was ripe." One broken promise followed another, but the Führer remained almost godlike.

From time to time attempts were made on Hitler's life. A few heroic Germans felt so strongly that the evil rule must end that they tried to kill him, knowing well they would pay with their own lives. Either from mischance or mismanagement each attempt failed. Built up by Nazi propaganda, the legend grew that Hitler had a charmed life.

In the spring of 1941 Nazi triumphs in Greece and Yugoslavia got great publicity, but the German people were far more interested in the later attack on Russia. They had been taught to hate and fear the Soviets, so the "Crusade Against Communism" was fairly popular. If the "Jewish Bolshevik" could be stamped out by a brief summer campaign, they were wholeheartedly for it.

By the winter of 1941 things were not nearly so cheerful on the Nazi home front. People had been surprised and disappointed when the summer passed without a major Russian defeat. They were shocked when Goebbels launched an urgent appeal for warm clothing for the troops on the Eastern Front. This was the first real sign of crisis.

News of the casualties began to come through. No official lists were published, but almost every family had someone fighting in the East, and they compared notes. Letters from the troops were heavily censored and very slow, and anxiety deepened.

Then another blow fell: Japan attacked Pearl Harbor, and the United States joined Britain and Russia against Germany. Many Germans had visited the United States and respected her industrial strength, so that now they knew that they were in for a long war.

Rations decreased, and the Germans had to tighten their belts; the number of *ersatz* (substitute) products rose.

Long before the war Hitler had tried to make Germany self-supporting by manufacturing substitutes for the things that she had to import. Clothes were made from wood pulp. They were neither as warm nor as hard-wearing as wool, and they shrank when they got wet. Men remarked sourly that if you started the winter with a pair of trousers, you had shorts all ready for the summer.

Shoes were made of ersatz leather. They did not keep out the rain, but it was necessary to register with a shoemaker to get them at all.

The Germans were never starving. Because of their European conquests, they were able to draw on surrounding countries to brighten up the monotony of Nazi larders. They lacked only the luxuries that had to be grown overseas. "Domestic herb tea" made from nettles appeared on the shelves, together with acorn coffee; ersatz chocolate was wrung out of wood pulp and eaten without much relish.

More and more men were called up to fill the gaping holes on the Eastern Front. Millions were imported from the occupied countries and used in factories as slave labor.

In 1942 the inhabitants of the big cities like Berlin, Hamburg, and Bremen were beginning to suffer seriously from the bombing. Air raid shelters were built, but the casualties were heavy and whole districts devastated. The German reaction was very like the British. People were desperate and angry, but not afraid. It was proved by both sides that civilian bombing does not break the spirit of a brave people.

In Berlin huge underground bunkers were built to protect Hitler. Despite his so-called charmed life he did not care to take chances.

In the summer of 1942 the world was shocked by one of the most ghastly of all the Nazi atrocities. It occurred in one of the occupied countries, for it was in those that the iron hand of the Gestapo had always fallen hardest.

Ever since the German occupation in 1939, Czechoslovakia had been a tough nut for the invaders to crack, for the Czechs are independent by nature, and they resisted the Nazi oppression with dogged perseverance. At the time when arms were being rushed to the Eastern Front clever sabotage in Czech factories caused repeated delays. Faulty weapons kept appearing from the Skoda works, guns jammed and bombs did not explode, and the trains carrying them to the front were involved in mysterious collisions.

Determined to discipline the Czechs, Hitler appointed the SS General Reinhard Heydrich to take charge of the situation in Prague. He had been sent to other troubled areas as an executioner, and had an unrivaled reputation for cruelty. In Prague he went to work without mercy or justice.

One day Heydrich was driving back to Prague after some act of punishment when a truck swung across the road in front of his car; at the same time two young men sprang onto the car and shot Heydrich, who died a week later.

Nazi reprisals were instantaneous. Whole families were taken out and shot without the slightest proof of guilt. A reward of ten million Czech crowns was offered for information which would lead to the capture of the culprits. When this failed to buy their betrayal, the reward was increased to twenty million — with no better results.

Finally the guilt was fixed on the little mining village of Lidice. Evidence shows no clear proof that anyone there was sheltering the men the Nazis were looking for. The village was chosen at random as a warning.

On June 9 squads of SS commandos, troops specially selected and trained to carry out atrocities, drove into the village. They assembled the entire population in the village square, the priest and the schoolmaster, the very young and the very old alike. Every single man over the age of eighteen was taken from his family, lined up, and shot. The stricken women were sent to concentration camps, their children torn away for Nazi "education" and their homes destroyed. Out of the five hundred inhabitants, not one remained alive in Lidice. The village lay plundered and deserted.

The news of the massacre of Lidice was broadcast over the Nazi radio. A great wave of horror and indignation swept over the free world.

In Illinois, the people of a little town lying in the green Mississippi River Valley changed its name to Lidice. They were determined that the name and the deed should not be forgotten.

Through its martyrdom Lidice has become immortal.

After the war was over, twenty-two of the most powerful Nazi leaders were tried before an international court at Nuremberg and cited as war criminals. The court was made up of the most prominent judges from America, Britain, Russia, and France. Each of the accused was defended by a counsel of his own choice; he could call witnesses and speak in his own defense. They were charged with responsibility for the war and with mass murder and cruelty. The terrible truth of Nazi crimes and atrocities was presented to the world. Twelve of the men (including Göring) were sentenced to death, four to long-term and three to life imprisonment. Three were acquitted.

Many men and women who had worked for the Nazis, spreading misery and terror in so many lands, were also tried, either by the Allies in the zones which they occupied for a time after the war or, in countries like Norway, by their own people. From official records, from eyewitnesses' accounts and from their own statements the evidence was collected and the verdicts given. They had the opportunity to prove their innocence — an opportunity which had not been granted to millions of their victims.

22

Free Men Fight Back

GERMANY WENT to war to enslave other nations. The United States, Britain, the Commonwealth, and France were forced into war to preserve their liberty from a monstrous tyranny.

They were not prepared for war either in their minds or with their weapons. Once they were roused they fought magnificently, but they had not wanted to fight at all. On the home fronts in the United States and Britain the people hated war, but in their different ways they set to work to beat Hitler.

In Britain, as the Battle of the Atlantic surged around the supply lines, rations shrank, for food was only a small part of the cargoes that came through the blockade. By 1943 cupboards were very bare. People were allowed a meat ration equal to two chops a week and only one egg. They stood in line for hours for a pound of fish. Clothing coupons covered only the bare necessities. "Bundles for Britain," packed in every city and town in America, were opened with joy and used with gratitude.

In America there were shortages too. Gasoline, tires, and most kinds of food were rationed. But because of the richness of the land and the industry of the people, there was always enough to go around. After the fall of Singapore Americans learned to produce synthetic rubber.

The tale is told of an English Sunday-school teacher who saved her butter and jam rations for a week and invited her two best pupils to tea. She bought three large buns. At the last moment a lonely little evacuee from London appeared in the class, and with Christian charity she invited him too. The children arrived, and the best scholar was asked to say grace. Bowing his head he said:

> Long to reign over us
> Three buns 'tween four of us
> Good job there's no more of us
> God save the King.

American families, with generous sympathy, took British children into their homes to protect them from danger. They went to school with American children, and lasting friendships grew up.

Both sides of the Atlantic had acute labor problems. Men and women were needed for the armed forces, the merchant navy, civil defense, hospitals, transport, and for the vast, expanding force of industrial workers.

In Britain conscription controlled both men and women. People's lives were no longer their own; they were caught up in the war machine. Women did jobs that they would have thought impossible before the war — and did them well. Queen Elizabeth II, then Princess Elizabeth, joined the ATS (Auxiliary Territorial Service) when she was eighteen, went into khaki and drove a truck.

In America women volunteered for the services. They enrolled in the Women's Army Corps (WAC), the Women's Air Force Service Pilots (WASP), and in the Navy's Women Appointed for Voluntary Emergency Service (WAVES). They served as nurses at home and with the armed forces all over the world. They went into industry to fill the places of men who had enlisted. Aircraft factories were the first to take on widows of men who had been killed at Pearl Harbor. Other plants followed, and soon women were working in factories throughout the country.

The industrial miracle of the Second World War was just shaping. Goods for lend-lease orders had been increasing monthly, but after Pearl Harbor the pace of production outstripped the planners' wildest dreams. The Allies had seen the overwhelming success of Nazi and Japanese attacks. Continental Europe and most of Asia had been crushed by sheer speed and firepower. Now America had to provide her forces with arms that would prove even more deadly.

President Roosevelt had said of his allies: "They

need tanks, guns, ammunition, and supplies of all kinds. They shall get them." And they had to be good. A factory worker on a propaganda poster expressed the proud promise: "You name it. We'll make it."

From small businesses to giant corporations everything switched from peace to war. Donald Nelson became a dynamic chairman of the War Production Board, and government and private industry worked together. Plants stopped making sewing machines, jukeboxes and refrigerators and were retooled for aircraft and tanks, bombs and shells, guns and jeeps. They turned out thousands of the new amphibious DUKWs, commonly called "ducks," that traveled either on land or sea. In the Detroit area in 1938 firms made nearly three million passenger cars; in 1944 they produced six hundred and ten.

Workers had to learn new techniques, and volunteers had to learn war trades. Factories were filled with students — "in the plant" schools enrolled training groups made up of schoolteachers and clergymen, farmers and professional baseball players, musicians and road menders, and entire troupes of Broadway entertainers.

There was a sudden migration from the shores of the East and West coasts to the vast stretches of the midlands. Factories sprouted in Colorado, Missouri, Utah, Mississippi, Nebraska, and Kansas. Agricultural land was submerged by cranes and sprawling sheds.

A new method of production grew. Parts of a

single machine were made at factories hundreds of miles apart and gathered with exact precision onto one great assembly line. Two hundred and forty-eight factories combined to make a Flying Fortress, and the atom bomb was created in laboratories and plants all over America.

Steel is the basis for modern arms, and in 1942 there was not enough for Allied needs. New diesel scoops were sent to the Great Lakes to gouge out the rough, red iron ore. It was carried by boat and train, thousands of miles, to mighty blast furnaces and coke ovens in the East, and new steel mills were built to finish the process. In 1944 America produced more steel than all Hitler's Europe together.

Oil was another war essential. All the oil that was used in Britain by the Allied air forces from 1942 onward was pumped from American wells. To carry the oil from the Texas fields to the refineries in the East, a pipeline was built. It was a gigantic project, but it took only three hundred and fifty days to complete, snaking across the wide plains and over the Allegheny Mountains to the Atlantic seaboard. Hundreds of thousands of barrels of oil passed through every day.

American shipbuilding in the Second World War was the most extensive ship construction ever known — warships to fight the enemy and merchant ships to carry troops and supplies. The war effort hung on its success. No numbers of guns and bombs were any good if they did not reach the battle front.

The building program had to beat the Nazi sinkings. New techniques were invented; welding replaced riveting. The Liberty ships and the name of Henry Kaiser became world famous. Before the war it had taken seven months from the laying of the keel to the launching of the ship. Men learned to do it in forty-one days. At the time of Pearl Harbor two merchant ships were launched in American yards every week; by 1943 six and a half ships were built every day and by 1944, fifty.

In this year production reached such a peak that American factories also turned out a plane every five minutes and eight aircraft carriers each week — to the dismay of the Nazis and the Japanese.

When a landing in Europe and the reconquest of the Pacific Islands was planned, landing barges received first priority. They were a brand-new necessity of modern warfare.

Millions of men had to be carried into shallow waters in the face of enemy fire. Andrew Jackson Higgins, a builder of small boats in New Orleans, invented a new design of shallow-draft boat. Orders flowed in from the Navy, and his shipyards were too small to carry them out. He roped off streets in New Orleans, strung up lights and, working through the twenty-four hours, built the boats and filled the orders.

Every American slipway was put into use. Shipyards along the coast and on riverbanks all over the country built landing barges. They were launched and floated down to the ports to be finished off.

The battle fought by American industry ended in overwhelming victory. The fine factories were not mangled by bombing, and the workers were not killed at work or in their homes, as they were in Britain. So the full capacity, skill, and patriotism of a free nation flowed out along the assembly lines.

In December 1941 Britain had gained a great ally. The country was soon studded with United States air bases, and the sky throbbed with the comforting roar of Liberators and Flying Fortresses. American bulldozers poked their snub noses into the rubble and cleared bomb damage. American troops poured into the country.

The radio was the core of wartime life, and people tried to hear every news bulletin. An English traitor called "Lord Haw-Haw" broadcast from Germany, giving the British people twisted versions of news about themselves. At first it was worrying, then it became ridiculous.

In Tokyo an American traitor followed suit. A female Haw-Haw, "Tokyo Rose," broadcast to American forces fighting in the Far East. She played old jukebox favorites, and did everything she could to make the GI's homesick.

London became a junction of free men. Patriots who refused to accept the puppet government which the Nazis established in their countries gathered there. Poles, Czechs, Norwegians, Dutch, Yugoslavs, Greeks, Belgians, and French set up headquarters. They fought gallantly on every front and every ocean along with American and British forces.

After the United States and Russia entered the war, Winston Churchill said:

We must remember that we are no longer alone. We are in the midst of a great company. Three-quarters of the human race are now moving with us. The whole future of mankind may depend upon our actions and upon our conduct. So far we have not failed. Let us move forward steadfastly together into the storm and through the storm.

So grew the Grand Alliance and later the fellowship of the United Nations.

23

Bombing Around the Clock

HITLER WAS BLINDED by the early success of the Luftwaffe. In 1940 he could not see that the tide of horror he had unleashed over Europe might turn to swamp his own people. He gloried in his blitz and ignored the possibilities of a boomerang.

In the Battle of France the bomber squadrons of the R.A.F. suffered heavy losses. During the summer of 1940, those that remained were kept busy breaking up Hitler's invasion craft and wrecking communications leading to the coast. On September 7 the blitz on London started, and on September 23 the first return raid on Berlin was carried out by British bombers. It was too small to do much harm, but it showed that the R.A.F. meant business, and a great surge of relief was felt by bombed Londoners.

As the Luftwaffe spread its trail of fire and havoc over Britain, the strength of Bomber Command gradually grew. Soon, in factories all over the country, men and women were working day and night making bombers to attack Germany.

By the beginning of 1942 the United States and British governments had traveled a long way from the "peace at any price" policy of 1938. Hitler had stirred up forces of resistance and retaliation that he had not known existed. War struck Germany from the air long before the Allied armies crossed her frontiers.

Since the war sharp criticism and heated argument have arisen over the right and wrong of Allied bombing of industrial targets, regardless of civilian suffering. But at the time when the British Empire, the United States, and Soviet Russia were losing millions of men, and fighting for their survival against the crushing onslaught of the Axis powers, the policy seemed necessary and right.

In February 1942 Air Chief Marshal Harris took over Bomber Command of the R.A.F. From then on, the German cities learned the full meaning of the kind of war Hitler had planned. The German people could not escape the tragic consequences of their choice of leader. City after city took, in increasing measure, the punishment that had befallen Coventry. Early in 1942 General Spaatz, who had been in England as an observer during the Battle of Britain, returned to take command of the American Eighth Air Force and later the Ninth Air Force in the Middle East. In a steady procession, Flying Fortresses and Liberators crossed the Atlantic under their own power, and touched down on the newly made airfields. Soon they joined the Stirlings, Halifaxes, and Lancasters in the assault on Nazi Europe.

German industry was centered in the Ruhr Valley, between the Rhine and Germany's eastern frontier. In this small area coal mines, iron and steel factories, synthetic oil plants, and armament factories combined to feed Hitler's war machine. The Ruhr was the arsenal of Nazi might.

Since Friedrich Krupp had made a few guns in a small forge at Essen a hundred years before, the town had grown to be the heart of armament production in Europe. In 1942 the Krupp plant was turning out munitions faster than any other factory in the world.

This was the first Ruhr target for Allied bombers. Hidden by a heavy cloud of black fog, the Ruhr Valley provided its own smoke screen.

In March 1942 the first big R.A.F. raid was launched against Essen. By long and careful experiment, Bomber Command had worked out a system of accurate attack through the haze. First Mosquito bombers, directed by radio, dropped indicator flares leading to the target. Then came the Pathfinders on their dangerous task to drop more indicator flares and some high-explosive bombs. Braving the antiaircraft fire and enemy night fighters, the Pathfinders stayed in the target area during the whole raid. They kept the target alight for the main bomber force which came over in waves with high explosives and clouds of incendiaries.

The system worked. By morning, when the fires

died down, acres of the Krupp plant lay in ruins. Many other factories were badly damaged, and whole districts of the town were laid waste. Thousands of people were killed, injured, or made homeless. This was the first blow in the Battle of the Ruhr. The people sampled the misery that was to beset them during the next three years, as one town after another shared the fate of Essen.

The Allies divided the bombing missions. The United States Air Force was trained for precision bombing by day. The R.A.F believed that massed raids by night were more deadly. So the Americans attacked particular strategic targets, while the R.A.F. set out to demolish the industrial cities. It was the beginning of the "around the clock" bombing that grew in ferocity as the strength of the Allies waxed and that of Germany waned.

The Battle of the Ruhr was fought with fury on both sides. The Germans brought in night fighters, and a forest of antiaircraft guns was planted over the whole area. Allied losses mounted dangerously, but the air crews pressed home their attacks with determination.

The industrial valley of the Ruhr, crammed with factories and swarming with workers, was supplied with water and electric power by three lakes: the Möhne, Eder, and Sorpe. Each lake held millions of gallons of water, and each was contained by a great concrete dam. If these dams could be breached, havoc would hit the valley below.

A plan that needed the utmost skill and daring

grew in the minds of men at Bomber Command Headquarters. They set out to form a squadron of "dambusters."

Wing Commander Guy Gibson, D.S.O. and Bar, D.F.C., was one of the most distinguished bomber pilots in the R.A.F. He had repeatedly proved his skill and courage. He was chosen to lead the operation, which was so secret that at first even he did not know the target.

Guy Gibson was given the pick of Bomber Command. He was told to collect the finest pilots and air crews he could find. So Squadron X was born, made up of Americans, Australians, Canadians, New Zealanders and British, each man selected for his particular skill and high resolve. They assembled at Scampton air station in Lincolnshire, none of them knowing where they were bound.

The training was new and hard. They took off each day at early dawn. Diving to treetop level, they skimmed lakes, reservoirs, and rivers. They practiced low flying endlessly, dropping their bombs at a hundred and fifty feet.

A scientist named Barnes Wallis designed a special type of bomb for the dambusters; nothing like it had ever been made before. On the trial runs the bomb burst too early, and Wallis set to work again in a frenzy of research. He found that if the bomb was to blast its way through a hundred feet of solid concrete, it must be dropped at precisely sixty feet. So the squadron lowered their flying level and learned to control their Lancasters at sixty feet. It was desperately low.

Bomber Command calculated that the greatest damage would result when the dams were full. While the training went on and the scientists toiled, the water rose, and observers reported the levels.

After a month of training Gibson was told his destination. He studied models of the dams and laid his plans. On May 16 the water in the dams reached its highest point, and the word was given to attack the next day. Gibson briefed his crews in extreme secrecy. Guards were posted and the camp sealed.

On May 17, 1943, as dusk fell, the eighteen Lancasters took off. They winged their way across the North Sea in a darkening sky and crossed the Dutch coast. They flew very low to escape night fighters. Two aircraft had trouble and were forced to turn back. The other sixteen reached Germany, hedgehopping all the way, and soon picked up the gleaming ribbon of the Rhine River.

They swung down to the Ruhr Valley, heading for the Möhne lake. It looked grim and cold in the moonlight, and the dam stood out in its massive strength. As Guy Gibson came in to make the first run, streams of flak spurted from the defenses around the dam. He held his course straight through the blinding barrage and dropped the first bomb. Huge sprouts of water rose and dashed over the face of the dam.

The squadron circled until the lake was calm.

Then one by one they went in to attack. Gibson flew in alongside each Lancaster, drawing the anti-aircraft fire. The bombs burst against the wall of the dam with tremendous upheavals, but it held. At the sixth attempt a great shout rose from the crews in the circling squadron. The stone face of the dam crumpled up and folded over.

The squadron flew on to the Eder dam, fifty miles away. A dull glow in the sky warned them of the dawn — time was running out. This was a much more difficult target; set in a steep valley, ringed by rocky peaks, the Eder dam seemed to defy destruction.

The Lancasters screamed down between the mountains and banked up sharply to avoid disaster. They tried again and again until they had only one bomb left. This was the last chance. The Australian pilot, Les Knight, made a perfect bomb run. In Gibson's words: ". . . as if a gigantic hand had punched a hole through cardboard, the whole thing collapsed." The squadron followed the great wall of water down the valley, and, as the dawn broke, they turned home.

They had no time and no bombs to breach the Sorpe dam, but it was a lesser target.

Of the sixteen aircraft in the attack, eight returned. Of the fifty-six men in the missing aircraft, only two survived. Men stood little chance at sixty feet.

Guy Gibson added the V.C. to his other honors, for his leadership and heroism. Although he had completed his flying duty he refused to be grounded; and in 1944, as a Master Bomber, he was shot down over Germany and killed.

By July 1943 the Ruhr defenses were taking a heavy toll of Allied bombers. The time had come to change the target. The most important shipbuilding yards in Germany lay in the port of Hamburg. Half the U-boat output came from these yards.

On the night of July 24 the R.A.F. struck. Seven hundred and forty bombers attacked in successive waves for two and a half hours. The defenses of the city were saturated with high explosive and incendiary bombs, and the German radar was confused by the dropping of metallic strips from the planes.

The damage was catastrophic. Gas and water mains were broken, electric power failed and the civil defense system broke down in panic and disorder. When morning came a deathly pall of smoke settled over the stricken city.

This was the beginning. During the next ten days the Americans sent over small precision bomber forces by day, and the R.A.F. huge forces by night.

Gigantic fires raged through the city. Set up by the intense heat, a gale of suction swept through the streets with irresistible force, drawing everything in its path towards the blazing furnace. People and their possessions were engulfed in the flames, and those who survived the ordeal fled to the country.

By August 3, two thirds of Hamburg lay in ruins; forty thousand people had been killed and about as many injured, and over five hundred factories were wrecked. Only in Dresden in the spring of 1945, and later with the atomic bomb, were death and destruction so overwhelming.

Before the end of the war almost every city and town in Germany had been bombed. The only way out for the German people was unconditional surrender, and that their war lords would not permit.

At the beginning of 1944 General "Hap" Arnold announced that his aircraft had dropped a million tons of bombs on Axis targets and his fliers had destroyed twenty-seven thousand enemy planes. And in March of the same year American bombers took their turn with the R.A.F. in bombing Berlin. The Berliners had feared this moment.

In the autumn of 1944, when the Allied armies were fighting in France, their bombers struck German oil to cripple the Nazi war machines. The skies over Germany flickered with the leaping flames rising from the synthetic oil plants, refineries and storage tanks. Millions of gallons of oil went up in smoke. The fires burned for days and showed the way to new squadrons. By the end of the year there was hardly a German refinery in full production.

To cut off other supplies the American Ninth Air Force, based in Egypt, had blitzed the refineries of Ploesti in Rumania. It was a long and dangerous mission — twenty-four hundred miles of flying — and the oil was heavily guarded by antiaircraft guns. If the gunners were surprised by the leading group they were thoroughly alerted for the arrival of the following bombers. Colonel Leon W. Johnson and Colonel John R. Kane won Medals of Honor over Ploesti. They led in their squadrons, placed third and fourth in the attack, through a blinding wall of fire and successfully completed their missions. In the same raid Major John Jersted had volunteered to lead a formation. Three miles from Ploesti his aircraft was hit and set on fire. He could have made an emergency landing, but he kept on to the target and dropped his bombs. His aircraft, now out of control, plunged into the flames. He too was awarded a Medal of Honor.

By the spring of 1945, when the Russian armies were sweeping in from the east and the Allies had crossed the Rhine, bombing brought German transport to a standstill. Railroads, bridges, repair shops, and marshaling yards lay in tangled masses of bent and splintered metal.

Those Ruhr factories which had managed to get back to work were useless. The railroads which should have taken the arms to the fronts were clogged with wreckage. Charred trucks and shattered engines littered the sidings. By this time the Luftwaffe was powerless to hinder the havoc.

It can never truly be said that the bombing broke the heart of the German people. Their courage and their industry did not fail. They endured life among ruins that have seldom been equaled. Even industrial production went on. Repairing the damage as best they could, the Germans worked with determination until the end.

Thousands of the best and bravest young Allied airmen were lost over Germany. The bombing of civilians was not an aim in itself: it was part of a life-and-death struggle to resist the evil Nazi conquest. It can only go down in history as part of the pitiless pressure of total war.

24

The Fall of Mussolini

Early in 1943 the North African battle was drawing to a victorious close, the German Sixth Army under General von Paulus was trapped in Stalingrad, and the Japanese had taken some hard knocks in the Pacific. The United States and Great Britain had been fighting side by side for a year. The Grand Alliance had come to pass.

The urgent question of striking at the heart of Nazi Germany by a cross-Channel invasion of France from British ports took first place in every Allied war council. Stalin was growing impatient at Allied delay, but he had mainly commanded land and air forces, and he had no idea of the complication of such a vast sea-borne landing. It was a gigantic project, and it had to succeed. Failure would set the Allies back for years and give Hitler a new lease on life.

With the Tunis victory in sight President Roosevelt, Mr. Churchill and their Chiefs of Staff met at

Casablanca in North Africa to plot the course of the war. The trip was a tremendous venture for the President. At Casablanca the Allied leaders decided to put off the Normandy landing until 1944 and to tackle Sicily and Italy first, the "soft underbelly of the Axis beast," as Winston Churchill put it.

A few months after the conference, in May 1943, North Africa was cleared of enemy forces and the Mediterranean opened to Allied shipping. For the first time since Italy had entered the war three years before, merchant ships unloaded their cargoes in the Grand Harbor of Malta without meeting a deluge of fire.

The way was cleared for the next battle, the invasion of Sicily — "Operation Husky." Warships and troop carriers, landing craft, and supply ships were collected off Malta. Airfields in North Africa and Malta were stocked with bombers, fighters, transport planes, and gliders. Troops were assembled and trained for the invasion. They were taught how to use the landing craft, such as the LSTs (Landing Ship, Tank) and "ducks."

General Eisenhower remained the Supreme Commander of the Allied Forces in the Mediterranean and General Alexander his second in command. General Montgomery commanded the British Eighth Army and General Patton the American Seventh Army. It was a strong team.

About forty miles south of Sicily, directly in the path of invasion, lay the Italian island fortress of Pantellaria. It was called the "Gibraltar of the central Mediterranean," and Mussolini boasted that it was unconquerable.

Nature had helped in the defense of the strong point. Formed of volcanic rock, the cliffs rose sheer from the sea to lofty, frowning peaks. A narrow mouth led to the one small harbor, and the surrounding heights were studded with tiers of guns set into caves deep in the solid rocks. The island was garrisoned by ten thousand Italian troops. There was little hope of blasting them out; but by this time the Italian forces were heartily tired of war, and the Allies thought that a dose of bombing might persuade them to surrender.

So for six days and six nights nonstop, from sea and air, the island was bombarded. The garrison was given no chance to sleep or repair the damage. Six cruisers and ten destroyers lay off and shelled the island, and bombers attacked ceaselessly. At the point when Allied troops were climbing into landing craft to make an assault, the fortress suddenly bristled with white flags. The first Fascist bulwark was in Allied hands.

Then the great Allied armada massed for the invasion of Sicily, the Italian island close to southern Italy. Admiral Cunningham, Commander in Chief of the British Mediterranean fleet, directed naval operations. The Italian fleet did not put in an appearance. Their battleships had been damaged in a Fleet Air Arm attack on Taranto harbor, and the fleet had taken a bad beating from Admiral Cunningham at Matapan during the Greek campaign.

Since then they had attacked convoys but had kept at a respectful distance from the main Allied fleets.

On the eve of the invasion the weather broke. The fleet was poised for action, aircraft and gliders lining the runways, when a storm whipped the Mediterranean into a whitecapped fury, beating in on the Sicilian beaches.

At his headquarters in Malta General Eisenhower was handed the weather reports. The wind force mounted steadily. The suspense was acute. It was too late to postpone the invasion; the distant transports had already sailed. At this stage the danger of putting it off would have been even greater than the danger of going ahead. The Commander in Chief gave the signal for the troops to go in.

At early dawn on July 10, 1943, the first units landed in Sicily. The armies were split into three sectors — the Americans on the west, Canadians in the center and the British on the east.

Off the beaches the sea teemed with shipping. The transports stood away from the shore while the landing craft plied to and fro. Destroyers and corvettes ranged busily around the fringe, alert for enemy interference. Overhead, Allied bombers passed on their way to harass enemy movements. Fighter squadrons screened the troop carriers as they came in to land. Invasion on such a scale had never been known before.

The Americans handled their landing with superb seamanship in heavy seas, on the windward side of the island. Their craft rode out the breakers, and the men landed with full equipment and moved swiftly inland. Parachute units were widely scattered in the high wind, but General Patton collected his Seventh Army after their stormy passage and made a wide westward sweep. Speed was Patton's slogan. He never gave the enemy time to recover from the shock of the invasion. With swift decision and excellent armor he confused their command and surrounded their units. Nazi troops fought under stern discipline, but thousands of Fascists surrendered, thankful to find a way out of the war. Then Patton swung eastward to join Montgomery's forces. Together they fought in the sweltering Sicilian plain and along the steep lava fields of Mount Etna.

The British and Canadian troops of the Eighth Army under Montgomery had had a tough time against German units. As the Nazis retreated they wrecked every road and bridge. The Allied armies were checked while engineers threw up trestle bridges to carry armored divisions on the narrow ledges between Mount Etna and the sea. Tanks and trucks swayed perilously on overhanging precipices skirting deep chasms. The infantry clambered up the treacherous slopes, clearing the enemy from clefts and gullies, in the face of constant sniping.

At last, on August 17, the Allied armies entered the town of Messina. Most of the German troops had escaped over the narrow sea straits to the mainland of Italy, closely pursued by Montgomery and the Eighth Army. After thirty-eight days of fierce fighting Sicily had been conquered.

The Allied invasion had a profound effect in Rome, for few Italians had been enthusiastic about the war into which they had been led by Mussolini. Now they wanted to get rid of him and finish the war as soon as possible, but they were hemmed in by the Nazis and surrender was difficult. So the anti-Fascists sent a secret agent to Lisbon to make contact with the Allies and discuss peace.

On July 25, while the Allied armies were fighting through Sicily, the Fascist regime collapsed. After twenty-two years of dictatorship Mussolini was dismissed both by King Victor Emmanuel and by his own party. He was forced to resign and was thrown into prison.

Hitler acted without hesitation: he sent one of his generals and a small detachment of SS troops to snatch Mussolini from jail. He set him up in the north of Italy — a puppet dictator with no power and no one to dictate to, living in sham grandeur.

The elderly King, the rightful head of the Italian State, had not actively organized fascism, but he had tolerated it and had lived on in Rome. Now he took over in place of Mussolini and appointed a Prime Minister, Marshal Badoglio, whom the Duce had disgraced for his failure to beat the Greeks.

The armistice between Italy and the Allied powers had been signed early in September. To protect the Italians from German anger, it was agreed that news of the armistice would not be made public until the Allies could stage a powerful landing on the Italian mainland.

Italy had surrendered unconditionally. By the terms of the armistice she was to "work her way" as a "co-belligerent." This meant that she had to turn around and declare war on Germany and that she must give the Allies as much help as possible. The Italian armed forces agreed to fight alongside the Allies. In actual fact most of the Italian Army was caught in German-occupied Italy, and those who did not get out were too war-weary to be much good.

The Italian fleet was ordered to surrender at Malta and obediently steamed out of Spezia and Taranto. On the way the Germans sank the flagship, with the Italian Commander in Chief, but the rest of the ships hauled down their flags in Malta's Grand Harbor, which they had tried so hard to destroy.

Of the eighty thousand Allied prisoners in Italian hands, the Nazis carried off seventy thousand to German prison camps. The remaining ten thousand were helped to escape, sheltered and passed through the German lines by Italian families and the Italian partisans. At the risk of their own lives, the Italian patriots helped the men on their journey to freedom.

25

The Road to Rome

ONCE SICILY WAS conquered the Allied commanders laid their plans for a landing on the Italian mainland — "Operation Avalanche." They had little choice of landing ground, for it had to be near a big port and within range of the Allied fighter squadrons based in Sicily. It was clear to the Allies, and also to the enemy, that Salerno was the only possible place. Fighters could spend twenty minutes over the beaches before returning to refuel, and Naples was nearby.

General Eisenhower held no false hopes of an easy landing. The Germans had first-class troops in southern Italy, and the Salerno beaches were dominated by gun emplacements. But there was no alternative.

The day before the invasion the Italian armistice was announced. The Germans moved instantly, seizing the railroads and everything else in Italy which they needed to carry on the war. Under General Kesselring, one of Hitler's most forceful commanders, Nazi divisions were rushed to the front so that Italy, instead of slipping quietly out of the fighting, found herself the center of battle.

General Mark Clark led the Allied Fifth Army into Italy. The beaches stretched invitingly before the approaching landing craft, in a long even curve. But this was deceptive — they proved to be heavily mined and barricaded with barbed wire. Concealed guns covered the bay, each manned by a German crew, alert for the attack.

At 3:30 on the morning of September 9, 1943, the first men set foot on the Salerno beaches. When dawn broke the Allied troops had won a narrow slip of land verging on the olive and orange groves. The Americans took one end of the beaches and the British the other. Both had sent airborne troops behind the enemy lines. They swung down and immediately formed up into little knots of resistance before the Germans set on them.

From the first hour the German defenses hammered the beaches. Kesselring brought up his crack Panzer divisions, the Herman Göring and the Panzer Grenadiers. They attacked constantly. The armored spearheads drove with shattering force against the British sector, then the American.

The American Thirty-sixth Division was among the first units ashore. They were troops untried in battle, and they acquitted themselves magnificently. Their lines were pitifully thin, and every man fought to hold a yard of shell-swept beach. They won the day by sheer defiance of danger.

The British sector was reinforced by the famous

The campaign in Sicily and Italy

Seventh Armored Division — the Desert Rats — but there was little room to maneuver tanks.

Out in the bay stood the fleet, shelling the Germans over the heads of the attacking troops. At night the mortar ships slipped close inshore to pound the enemy lines. The sky was rent with blinding flashes.

Overhead the Allied air forces roared in a constant, throbbing drone.

Under cover of darkness the Luftwaffe attacked the ships. They dropped flares and followed up with bombs. When a tanker was hit the flames soared high, floodlighting the fleet and the beaches with terrifying brilliance. For the first time the Germans used radio-controlled glider bombs. They fell among the host of ships and did great damage.

After a week of battering attack by the German Panzer divisions the pressure slackened. The Allied troops deepened their foothold and, yard by yard, fought their way inland.

All this time General Montgomery, with the Eighth Army, had been fighting his way up from the pointed toe of Italy. Nine days after the Salerno landing he joined up with the Fifth Army, and together they prepared to break out of the beachhead.

The advance started in the slush and slime of the autumn rains. The Seventh Armored Division dug itself out of an olive grove and ground its way north. The Fifth Army, composed of American and British troops, made for Naples. The columns passed the ruins of Pompeii and skirted the great rumbling mountain of Vesuvius. The Bay of Naples, with the exquisite island of Capri, opened up before them.

They captured the port, and the bulldozers got to work on the docks. With a supply base behind them the Allied armies were strengthened. They fanned out across Italy, the Fifth Army taking the western side and the Eighth Army the eastern side towards the Adriatic Sea. Free French troops under General Juin and a Polish Brigade under General Anders joined the Fifth Army. Their front faced the wide reaches of the Volturno River, and behind that loomed the heights of Monte Camino and farther north the towering fastness of Monte Cassino.

A succession of rivers ran directly across the path of both armies. Every bridge had been destroyed in the German retreat; the banks were defended from the opposite side, and the streams were in torrential winter flood. The approaches were churned into swamps of deep, clinging mud, in which the armored divisions wallowed. It never seemed to stop raining. The troops spoke sarcastically of "sunny Italy." The broiling heat of the Sicilian plain was far behind them.

The Fifth Army crossed the Volturno on a broad front in the face of savage enemy attack. The engineers threw up bridges almost as the leading troops crossed. The speed and skill of American reconstruction under fire was a new force in battle. The armed bulldozers wound their ponderous way to the forefront of the fighting, where their giant strength worked wonders.

The Eighth Army reached the precipitous banks of the Trigno River, and to their joy and amazement the stone bridge was intact. But when a few men were across, the bridge was blown up by a time bomb, and the rest forced a costly passage. Ahead of them lay the River Sangro, for there was always another river.

Now the armies were up against the winter as well as the enemy; snow was falling in the mountains, and the valleys were filled with icy streams. Everywhere it was bleak and raw, and the troops were chilled to the bone.

At the end of 1943 General Eisenhower went to England to take supreme command of the Allied Expeditionary Forces. There he would direct "Operation Overlord," the main assault on the stronghold of Germany. General Montgomery went too, as Commander in Chief of the British Forces under Eisenhower. General Alexander assumed command in Italy, General Mark Clark continued to command the Fifth Army and General Leese took over the Eighth Army.

The armies in Italy never had enough men, for they were constantly being sent to other fronts. As soon as one battle was won, the next loomed just ahead, and with fewer troops they had to make even greater efforts. Their job was to hold down the greatest possible number of Germans with the fewest possible number of their own men, and with such small forces every man was strained to the utmost. By January 1944 they had fought for six months without rest or relief.

The men were weary but undaunted, and the examples of their gallantry are countless. Private Elden Johnson was advancing through a valley with his infantry company when they were ambushed. In order to allow his comrades to escape, Private Johnson braved the massed fire of about sixty German riflemen, three machine guns and three tanks. He stood erect at twenty-five yards' distance to draw the enemy fire. Before he fell, mortally wounded, he destroyed one of the machine guns. He was awarded the Congressional Medal of Honor for his courageous sacrifice.

In the same month on the Damiano Ridge, south of Rome, a German machine gun was causing severe casualties, so Private Mitchell of the London Scottish Regiment charged up the hill alone through heavy fire. He leapt into the gun pit, captured the gun and disposed of the gun crew. The advance proceeded, but again it met with withering fire. Private Mitchell led his section on to capture two more enemy positions and cleared the way for the unit to pass. He then continued to lead his section until he was shot dead by one of his prisoners. He was awarded the Victoria Cross.

While the Eighth Army battled in the east, the

Fifth Army was fighting in the mountains against German fortified positions. The Nazis commanded all the mountain passes from ramparts on the heights, and their gun emplacements, hewn out of sheer rock, were proof against air attack. The only way to capture them was by storming the ridges in the face of merciless fire, so the advance was slow and won at heavy cost. In two months' fighting the Fifth Army had advanced only ten miles, but they had conquered the two great bastions of Monte Camino and Monte Trocchio, mountain fortresses on the road to Rome.

In January a new enterprise was launched. General Alexander planned a landing behind the enemy lines to shake their front. In great secrecy a force set out by sea from Naples, bound for Anzio, on the coast between the German front and Rome.

In the beginning all went well, and the Germans were taken completely by surprise. The Allied troops won a firm bridgehead and brought in armor and supplies; but then the commanding officer paused instead of striking the disordered German forces at once. He attacked too late; instead of sweeping out to join the Fifth Army the garrison found itself sealed into a little strip, surrounded by an iron fence of German armor. With no saving cover, the Anzio troops were raked by close-range enemy fire and were pinned down, beating off violent tank attacks, for months on end.

Hitler sent a special order to General Kesselring

to smash the beachhead, but Kesselring could not carry it out. American troops bore the brunt of the Anzio battle, and they did not falter.

Monte Cassino towered in front of the Fifth Army like a sentinel guarding the way to Rome. The old Benedictine monastery, where the monks still lived and worshiped, crowned the mountain above the town. It lay in the center of German fortifications, surrounded by gun emplacements and a maze of strong points, and dominated the only pass through the mountains.

A solemn problem lay before General Alexander, for without an attack on the sacred monastery height he could not take his armies through the pass. Finally he warned the monks and reluctantly bombed the Cassino fortifications.

Then the Thirty-sixth Division, which had a splendid battle record at Salerno, was sent forward to attempt a crossing of the Rapido River at the foot of Monte Cassino. In the flooded valley, against murderous fire, with fearful casualties, the remnants of two companies reached the opposite bank. For forty-eight hours they clung to pinpoints of sodden ground, until their ammunition was exhausted.

Two days after this tragic failure General Clark ordered the American Thirty-fourth Division to another reach of the Rapido to force a crossing. Fred Majdalany tells us in his book *Cassino:*

First the approach across the flooded valley, then the wading of the icy river, then the pill-boxes, dugouts, caves and fortified houses along the lower slopes, and then — if they lived that long — they must fight up the mountains themselves. . . . That was the task of the Thirty-fourth Division.

They crossed the river and, always under fire, crawled their agonizing way up the bare, cratered slopes littered with their own dead. Day after day and night after night they clung to their gains. In the end the few survivors were relieved by the Fourth Indian Division and New Zealanders who had been brought in from the Eighth Army. Again Fred Madjalany writes:

The performance of the Thirty-fourth Division at Cassino must rank with the finest feats of arms carried out by any soldiers during the war. When at last they were relieved by the Fourth Indian Division, fifty of those who held on to the last were too numbed with cold and exhaustion to move. They could still man their positions but they could not move out of them unaided. They were carried out on stretchers and it was one of the cruelties of this battle that some of them, having survived so much, were killed on their stretchers by shell fire on their long, tortuous way down to safety.

Then the fresh troops tried to storm the height. The Indian division attacked first, in waves up the bare cliff; but wave after wave was wiped out before reaching the defenses. New Zealanders attacked next with equal heroism and equal losses. After a series of grueling assaults the Indians and New

Zealanders finally won a foothold in the town of Cassino, which had been flattened by Allied bombing during the long attack and looked as though a giant scythe had been at work. They thrust a thin wedge into the ruins and held it but were driven back from the monastery height.

The German armies had dug in on the Adolf Hitler Line, right across Italy, and the Allied troops were too exhausted to force a breakthrough.

In May 1944 the front came to life. In Cassino, a Polish brigade under General Anders stormed through the town and with matchless valor, in the face of deadly fire, charged repeatedly over the rubble and captured the commanding height. At last, after four grim months, Monte Cassino was in Allied hands and the way to Rome was opened.

At the end of May, with a grand offensive, the whole Allied front swayed forward. The troops broke out from the Anzio beachhead to join the advancing armies. The Adolf Hitler Line broke, and the Germans were in full retreat.

On June 4, 1944, the Allied armies entered Rome. Long columns of tanks and infantry filed under the great arches that Mussolini had built for his own glorification and on through the ancient streets of the Eternal City.

The troops were hailed with wild excitement and rejoicing by the Roman people. Carnival reigned in the city. It was the first European capital to be liberated from Nazi bondage, and it was a great victory.

The long, hard struggle from the Sicilian beaches, up the Italian peninsula to Rome had been a truly Allied action. American, British, Canadian, New Zealand, Indian, South African, French and Polish troops, fighting the stubborn battle side by side, all earned a share in the triumph.

26

The Underground Rebellion

THE NAZI SYSTEM never flourished outside Germany. Though Hitler set up his apparatus of terror in one country after another he was never able to break the spirit of the people. In France, Holland, Norway, Belgium, Luxembourg, Italy, Poland, Greece, and Yugoslavia, when the Panzer divisions rolled in, freedom went underground, but it did not die.

At first people were subdued, stunned by defeat; in any case they did not know what life under the Nazis would be like. As the invaders showed their true colors and the Gestapo got to work, the flame of resistance was kindled: patriots in every country, each in his own way, defied Nazi tyranny.

The Resistance had no bounds of nationality, race, creed, or political opinion. Men, women, boys and girls, rich and poor alike, fought the underground war. Lawyers and statesmen, doctors and teachers, cowboys and writers, farmers and factory workers, truck drivers and shopkeepers found their place in the shadow army.

In Washington the O.S.S. (Office of Strategic Services) was set up after Pearl Harbor. A top-secret service under Major General William Donovan, it collected information and sent out agents to fight an underground war behind enemy lines on every front.

Churchill's V-sign cropped up everywhere. In 1940 it had become familiar in England where its Morse sounds, dot-dot-dot-dash, were used to open broadcasts to the Continent. Sounded on train whistles, tapped out on café glasses, shrilled like the hoot of an owl and chalked up on walls, it was a symbol of resistance.

People who worked in the Resistance ran desperate risks. They were never free for an instant from the fear of arrest and the dread of torture, for the Gestapo stopped at nothing to gain the information they needed.

In the occupied countries men and women were racked and tormented to force them to betray their comrades, and although a few broke down most of them endured the long-drawn-out agony in silence. Many of them carried poison pills concealed in their clothing to end the suffering if it was more than they could bear. Many survived the inquisition, only to die in the horror of a concentration camp. The men of the O.S.S. ran the same risks.

Cruel reprisals fell on innocent families and on

whole villages suspected of helping the Resistance, but the work went on.

In France, from tiny centers of heroic actions, the Resistance grew into a network of underground rebellion.

When the newspapers were suppressed by Nazi orders, an underground press started up. Printed in secret on kitchen tables, in back rooms and cellars, the little papers were distributed among the patriots. The underground press rallied Free Frenchmen, correcting the Nazi lies and giving the people news of the war. In defiance of orders from the Vichy government and the Gestapo, millions of Frenchmen also listened to the British broadcasts.

Link by link, the chain of resistance grew, and leaders rose to direct the different groups all over the country.

In Paris the National Council of the Resistance was led by M. Bidault, who became Prime Minister of France after the war. In constant touch with General de Gaulle in London, the Resistance organized the sabotage of bridges, railways, and enemy installations from one end of France to the other.

The *Maquis,* bands of partisans operating in the hills and woods, lived hard and dangerously. They were short of arms and hungry most of the time. Cut off from their families for fear of reprisals they devoted their lives to harassing the enemy. The leaders of the Maquis traveled from one group to another, passing through the cordon of the Gestapo under different disguises and with forged identity cards.

In almost every town and village the Resistance built up loyal contacts. Doctors played an important part and partisans never lacked medical care if they were ill or wounded.

Radio operators kept in touch with Britain, transmitting and receiving messages with portable radios. They reported enemy movement and partisan plans and requirements, and were continually hunted by the Gestapo who ranged over the country with radio detectors. The operators often finished a vital message when their pursuers were within a few hundred yards.

Working with the O.S.S., the American Air Force and the R.A.F. dropped arms and secret agents to the French underground. They flew in at night to a secret rendezvous where the partisans were anxiously waiting. As the aircraft approached, men on the ground lighted flares around the reception area. When the parachutes had fluttered down bearing men and supplies, the flares were dimmed and all signs of the drop were quickly swallowed up in the darkness.

The Resistance in the occupied countries was powerless to prevent Hitler's putting factories and railways to work for the Nazi war effort. Allied leaders were deeply distressed at the thought of killing loyal friends in air attacks on enemy targets. Yet people in France, Belgium, Holland, Norway, and Italy accepted the raids with amazing courage and understanding. They knew that the sacrifice was a prelude to freedom. Working with the Resistance the Allied air forces made pinpoint attacks on very special targets.

Thousands of British and American airmen who had been shot down were smuggled out of France by the O.S.S. and the Resistance. Passed on from one family to another, they were hidden in cupboards and chests, pushed out of back windows while the Gestapo came in at the front door, sheltered and fed by their valiant hosts.

The partisans wasted no effort to annoy the Nazis in big or little ways. In Marseilles they went out at night and lifted the covers off the sewers; when the German troops returned to barracks through the darkened streets, after an evening in the bars and cafés, they fell through manholes and ended the evening bruised, filthy and very angry.

In Paris a crippled old lady was frequently seen hobbling up from the Metro (subway), waving her crutches uncertainly in an apparent effort to keep her balance. As one crutch swung wide a Nazi officer sprawled down the stairs. The old lady tottered on with a wicked grin on her face. *"C'est mon troisième aujourd'hui"* ("It's my third today"), she muttered under her breath.

Late in the war, after the Allied armies had landed in France, a wave of sabotage swept over the country; for arms had been hoarded for the moment of liberation. At one period General Eisenhower valued the work of the Free French Resistance as equal to many army divisions. They wrecked the German supply lines and paved the way for the advancing Allies so that the Germans never knew when they would be attacked from the rear. In Paris the patriots rose to liberate the city.

Nazi anxiety found an outlet in an act of insane vengeance. The village of Oradour-sur-Glane lies in the Massif Central, a stronghold of the Maquis, and Hitler sent an SS atrocity unit to search the village. They found no arms or evidence of resistance, but they murdered the people all the same. Every man was shot and the women and children locked in the church and burnt alive. Out of seven hundred people, only six survived.

In Norway the independent spirit of the people never faltered. Hitler's puppet, Major Quisling, and his smattering of Nazi followers held little power and were despised by most Norwegians.

Resistance was helped by the nature of the country. The Gestapo moved into Norway in force, but they could not patrol every forest and mountain or watch the whole coastline. When they combed the towns for labor for German factories, many men took to the open country and got away.

The Nazis tried to direct the children of Norway, but when the boys and girls were ordered to join the Nazi Youth Movement, none turned up. Children were taken to the Hitler Youth Exhibition in Oslo, but they walked around it with their eyes fixed on the ground.

Schoolteachers were ordered to teach German instead of English as a second language and to bring up the children on Nazi doctrines. The only result was that in February 1941 the teachers went out on strike. Hundreds of them were rounded up and sent to a concentration camp where they were starved and brutally ill-treated. Five hundred were crammed into the hold of a cargo ship and taken to the north of Norway, where they worked on the docks under terrible conditions. Flogged and starved, many died, but the rest held firmly to their beliefs. In the face of such determinations, Quisling was helpless. The schools reopened, and the old teaching went on. The Norwegian clergy, too, refused to spread the Nazi creed.

From their headquarters in Britain, King Haakon and his government kept in touch with the Norwegian Resistance, and in 1941 the contact was strengthened, when the "Shetland Bus" began to run. This was made up of a small fleet of Norwegian fishing boats that had escaped to Britain. The were assembled in the Shetland Isles and sailed regularly to Norway, manned by their Norwegian crews. It was a venturesome crossing for a small boat alone, but the Viking ships had made it many times, centuries before. They crossed the North Sea by night and mingled with other fishing boats off the Norwegian coast, to escape the attention of the Nazis. Mainly in winter, because of the long, dark nights, they carried out their dangerous missions through storm and blizzard.

The Shetland Bus took over arms and supplies and brought back Norwegian refugees and a great deal of valuable information. Traveling with forged documents, the Norwegians often managed to bluff the Gestapo when they were challenged. As fishing boats were lost, other crews volunteered to join the fleet.

In 1943 a tiny party of Norwegians was dropped on the bleak snow fields near the great hydroelectric plant at Vemork in southern Norway. This turned out Europe's largest supply of "heavy water," a highly concentrated substance essential for atomic research. It is very difficult to produce, and the main German supply came from Vemork.

The instructions of the invading party were to destroy the heavy-water machinery. To prepare for their job they lived for months in a mountain hut, cut off from human contact, very short of food, while they explored the land and laid their plans.

In April 1943 the nine men, armed with high explosives and traveling on skis, dashed down into the valley where the plant lay. With cool daring and precise skill they wrecked the complicated machinery before the German guards knew that anything was afoot. Heavy-water production at Vemork came to a standstill.

The following year Norwegian secret agents in the plant reported that Hitler had decided to transport the remains of the heavy water to Germany. He knew that if he could get it safely through, years of expensive and difficult research would be saved. The loss of this heavy water would fatally set back atomic progress in Germany.

So the little party of Norwegian guerrillas got going again, and this time they decided that the best chance of sabotaging the heavy water without grievous loss of Norwegian lives was to sink it on the train ferry near Vemork, the only route across the nearby fiord to Germany.

Units of special SS troops arrived to guard the drums of precious water, which were labeled with an innocent description and loaded on the train. Disguised as electricians, the saboteurs went aboard the ferry and laid the explosive with a time fuse. In the deepest part of the fiord the ferry blew up and sank. It had been impossible to warn the captain, and he and his Norwegian crew perished.

Hitler gave up hope of making an atom bomb.

Early in 1944 a unit of specially trained O.S.S. men landed by parachute on snow-covered mountains in northern Norway. Of the three transport planes which took off from Britain two crashed in a blinding blizzard. Of the original forty-two men only sixteen landed safely.

Joining up with loyal Norwegians, this tiny group set out over the mountains, bearing heavy loads of ammunition and explosives but very little food. Their targets were a bridge and junction on the Norwegian Nordland Railroad. With the temperature at twenty degrees below zero, sleeping in dugouts in the snow by day and moving on by night, constantly dodging Nazi patrols, they traveled on skis for over a hundred miles.

At this stage of the war Hitler faced an acute shortage of men, and recalled troops from every occupied country. The Nordland Railroad was the only connection between Germany and northern Norway, where there was a large Nazi garrison. With cool daring and organized stealth the O.S.S. saboteurs wrecked the railroad so well that for the rest of the war, with difficulty and delay, the Germans were forced to use an emergency line.

Holland suffered terribly from Nazi occupation. The Dutch people were concentrated in a small country. They had no wild land where they could go into hiding. There were no forests or mountains to shelter them, so that they were completely at the mercy of the Gestapo.

There were a great many Jews in Holland before the war, and many more fled there from Nazi persecution. By Hitler's orders they all wore a yellow star, the Star of David, to mark them out for special oppression. They were not issued ration cards, they had to keep a rigid curfew and they were not allowed to work for their living. From time to time thousands were rounded up and thrown into concentration camps.

Risking the same fate, the Dutch people carried on a stubborn resistance. When ration cards were denied to the Jews, the Resistance forged them;

when identity cards were needed to trick the Gestapo, they printed false ones; when the newspapers were suppressed, the editors produced underground editions; and when Jews were hunted down, members of the Resistance hid them in their own homes. Fugitives lived in hollowed-out haystacks, in caves under kitchen floors, in secret cupboards and in walled-up attics.

When American and British airmen were shot down over Holland, if they could make contact with the partisans, they got generous aid. Many of them were passed along the escape routes through Belgium and France to Spain and Portugal.

The Dutch Resistance reported that the Gestapo housed their records of patriot activities in a five-story house in The Hague, so the R.A.F. set out to destroy the records which condemned many Dutchmen to death. Wing Commander Bateson led his Mosquitoes in to attack. Flying at fifty feet, skimming the roof tops, he pounced on the Gestapo office. The bombs went in through the front door "as if they had been put down by hand," and the records were blown up and scattered. The work of the patriots continued. After the raid it was doubly difficult for the Gestapo to round them up, as a set of fake records had found their way into German hands. The Resistance had forged them specially to mislead and confuse the Nazis.

Dutch boys and girls played a gallant part in the underground work, for messages had to be carried through the Nazi patrols, food delivered to the people in hiding and the Resistance newspapers circulated. The responsibility and danger were very great. The teenagers took on the jobs, and putting on an act of carefree youth they passed unnoticed by the Nazi guards. They clattered for miles from village to village over the cobbled roads on bicycles without tires. They pushed their younger brothers and sisters in prams with concealed food for starving families. In winter they skated along the canals bearing warning of approaching danger.

Many children had fathers who were hiding to escape the Nazi labor gangs, and they learned not to talk. Their discipline and courage constantly defeated the Gestapo. The boys and girls in all the occupied countries learned, too, the full meaning of injustice and treachery.

Seyss-Inquart, Nazi Commissioner in Holland, was one of the twelve men sentenced to death at the Nuremberg Trials after the war; he was charged with supreme cruelty.

In Eastern Europe Hitler treated his conquests even more harshly than in the west, for they belonged to what he called the "slave races." In Poland the ruthlessness of the occupation forces roused the people to desperate acts of resistance and, with total disregard for danger, they built up an Army of Liberation under General Bor-Komorowski. In the summer of 1944, in the Warsaw Rising, the

Liberation Army and the Jewish people in Warsaw were wiped out with unspeakable savagery by the Nazi forces.

Farther south, in Greece, bands of partisans, mainly under Communist leadership, fiercely resisted German and Italian occupation. They set up headquarters in the rugged mountainous country, and despite merciless reprisals on the Greek people their acts of sabotage went on.

At a critical time in the war the main railroad bringing supplies through Greece to be shipped to the Nazi forces in the Western Desert was out of action. The partisans had wrecked the great Gorgopotamus viaduct by a might feat of sabotage. The viaduct had spanned a deep gorge, and it took the Germans months to rebuild it.

One of the best organized resistance movements in Europe was led in Yugoslavia, first by General Mikhailovitch who represented the legal government of Yugoslavia, and later by Marshall Tito, a Communist who had lived in Soviet Russia. Tito was determined to destroy the Nazis, overthrow the Yugoslav government and set up a Communist regime.

Tito was a forceful and fearless revolutionary leader. His name, meaning in Serbo-Croat "do this — do that" (*ti-to*), became a slogan for action. Tito's guerrilla bands, although ragged and poorly armed, grew into an army. They waged unrelenting war against the Nazi and Fascist occupation forces and against all those who opposed Tito's politics.

The Allies not only gave Tito air and naval support but also parachuted arms and supplies into his mountain strongholds. With the assistance of the Soviet Red Army, Tito and his forces recaptured Belgrade from the Germans and became the master of Yugoslavia which Tito soon transformed into a Communist State.

For five bitter years Hitler struggled, first by persuasion, then by persecution, to turn the people of the occupied countries into enthusiastic Nazis. He had defeated their armies by treachery and force, but the stubborn spirit of the ordinary people was beyond his power.

27

Victory in the Atlantic

THE STORM OF WAR had struck one country after
another. In somber succession each paid the heavy
price of Hitler's hate. But the longest and perhaps
most critical battle of all was the Battle of the
Atlantic.

The great sea actions of the war, with battleships,
aircraft carriers, and cruisers, were fought mainly
by the Americans in the Pacific and the British in
the Atlantic and Mediterranean. But the exhausting
and perilous task of shielding the Atlantic convoys
was shared by the escort fleets of the United States,
Britain, and Canada. For years victory or defeat
hung on their efforts.

From the first day of the war the violence of the
Nazi attack in the Atlantic rose steeply. By the
spring of 1941 the outlook for Britain was bad. The
Germans were building U-boats faster than they
lost them, and the British were losing ships faster
than they could build them.

The United States was not yet in the war, the French fleet was out of action and the Italians were attacking in the Mediterranean. Britain was forced to send her Far Eastern convoys on the long trip around the Cape of Good Hope, and was desperately short of ships.

In March 1941 lend-lease came into force; American shipyards built ships for Britain, and the "arsenal of the democracies" began to turn out weapons.

After the fall of Norway and Denmark British army units occupied Iceland to prevent Hitler from seizing a base from which he could straddle the seaways to Britain. A year later American troops relieved the British forces. From then on the United States Navy escorted convoys of merchant ships, laden with goods for Britain, which sailed from America to Iceland. Shipping of any nationality could join the convoys. In fact, seafaring hitch-hikers were welcome. After Iceland, British and Canadian warships took over the convoy duties and between them covered the remainder of the Atlantic route. The merchantmen and their escorts grew painfully familiar with the bleak outline and treacherous seas around their new northern base; but icebergs were better than U-boats.

When the United States declared war on Germany a new crisis arose, for Hitler sent his U-boat fleet to attack shipping off the shores of America. It was a U-boat paradise. All along the Atlantic coast traveled a rich stream of cargoes — meat from the Argentine, coffee from Brazil, grain and sugar from Puerto Rico and above all oil from Venezuela. No convoy system was yet in operation, and the merchant ships were defenseless. The U-boats carried out a wholesale massacre, going for the tankers first. The Allies lost more ships in 1942 than in any previous year.

Behind the widespread havoc of the U-boats lurked the menace of the two great Nazi super-battleships, the *Bismarck* and the *Tirpitz*. It was known early in 1941 that they were nearly ready to come into action. They were obviously designed to ravage Atlantic shipping.

Coastal Command of the R.A.F. kept anxious watch on their progress, and at Scapa Flow the British Home Fleet was held in readiness for battle. In May 1941 it was suddenly discovered that the *Bismarck's* berth was empty. She had slipped out under cover of low cloud and disappeared.

Admiral Holland, in his flagship *Hood,* with the brand new battleship *Prince of Wales* and two cruisers, *Norfolk* and *Suffolk*, put to sea in pursuit. After two days of acute tension the *Suffolk* sighted the *Bismarck* with the heavy cruiser *Prince Eugen* in attendance. The British battleships closed in and Admiral Holland attacked with the *Hood* and the *Prince of Wales*. The four great ships opened a gun duel, and the *Bismarck* scored a hit on the *Hood* amidships. With a colossal explosion the *Hood* blew up and sank in a few minutes. From her ship's company of 1,419 only three men were saved.

The *Bismarck* turned south, leaving a wake of oil from damaged fuel tanks, while the *Prince of Wales* signaled for reinforcements. The *Bismarck* was heading for the refuge of a French port; it was a race against time.

At dusk two days later, through a break in the clouds, Swordfish aircraft from the carrier *Victorious* spotted the *Bismarck*. In failing light, with stormy seas and low scudding clouds, aim was difficult, but the Swordfish drove home their attacks until a low-fired torpedo wrecked the *Bismarck*'s steering gear and jammed her rudders.

The battleships *George V* and *Rodney*, the cruiser *Dorsetshire* and a destroyer flotilla had now joined the *Prince of Wales*. Though crippled and out of control, the *Bismarck* could still use her powerful guns, and she fought the British ships all through the night. Her fate was sealed, but she did not surrender. Riddled with armor-piercing shells and belching black smoke, she fought until the *Dorsetshire* put in a torpedo amidships and finished the battle.

The *Bismarck* went down with her flag flying. The defiant courage of her captain and the might of her guns would have proved a terrible danger to Atlantic shipping, and the relief in Britain was immense.

One of the gravest responsibilities that the Allied navies undertook was the protection of troop convoys. By 1943 thousands of Americans were crossing the Atlantic each month bound for battle. In stormy weather the troopship *Dorchester* set out for Greenland, where the United States forces had a base. Just after midnight on February 3, 1943, she was torpedoed.

The bravery of the four chaplains on the *Dorchester* is an outstanding instance of supreme self-sacrifice. The *Dorchester* was sinking, and in the darkness there was panic and confusion. The four chaplains belonged to different religions: John Washington was a Catholic priest, Alexander Goode a Jewish rabbi, George Fox and Clark Poling were Protestants. They climbed around the slanting decks encouraging the men, helping them to abandon ship, and distributing life jackets. When the supply was exhausted each of the four chaplains gave up his own jacket, well knowing that without it there was little chance of survival in the icy water. As the ship went down they stayed on board speaking words of comfort and praying for the safety of their men. Each of the chaplains was awarded posthumously a Purple Heart and a Distinguished Service Medal.

In Philadelphia a chapel has been built to their memory, an inter-faith shrine with three altars, Catholic, Jewish and Protestant. It is open at all times to all people.

In this same year Germany lost many of her best U-boat commanders. Prien, who had sunk the *Royal Oak*, went down with his submarine, and other Nazi aces were either killed or captured. They were men who could not be replaced, and though the wolf pack attacks went on, the days of individual U-boat exploits were ending.

Now anxiety was focused on the second great battleship, the *Tirpitz*. Early in 1942 she began to move along the Norwegian coast, the jumping-off place for an attack, and other German warships joined her. The R.A.F. and the British Navy patrolled the North Sea constantly.

If the *Tirpitz* was damaged in battle the only dock outside Germany large enough to take her for repairs was at St. Nazaire in Brittany, the port to which the *Bismarck* had headed the summer before, after she was hit by the *Prince of Wales*. The British Admiralty decided that if Hitler could not get the *Tirpitz* repaired, he might not dare to send her into battle at all.

So a commando raid was planned to wreck the dock at St. Nazaire. Preparations began in the greatest secrecy at Falmouth in southwest England.

The men were put through strenuous training, but they were not told the aim and object of the exercise. Motor launches were fitted with special gadgets. The old American destroyer *Campbeltown* was docked, her funnels sloped to resemble those of German destroyers, her bow strengthened and then filled with five tons of high explosive. A rumor was spread that a big antisubmarine exercise was planned.

The raid was fraught with danger. St. Nazaire was the most heavily defended port in France. The commando force had to cross the Bay of Biscay, sail five miles up the narrow channel of the river Loire and drive the *Campbeltown* into the very center of the great dock gates. The slightest error in direction or timing meant complete failure.

The attack had to be carried out at high tide and the raiding forces cleared by 4 A.M., when dawn broke. On May 26 the tide was right and everything was ready. The commandos were briefed. When the *Campbeltown* had breached the gates they were to storm the docks and destroy the machinery and the pumping house. They were shown perfect miniature models of St. Nazaire, and each man knew exactly what he had to do.

The little fleet set out from Falmouth as dusk fell: sixteen motor launches, one motor gunboat, one motor torpedo boat, the *Campbeltown* and two escorting destroyers, the whole manned by six hundred and thirty men, about half of them naval.

At about 1 A.M. the following night they reached the mouth of the Loire. The weather, overcast with a slight drizzle, was good for the landing party but bad for the R.A.F., which went in first to create confusion among the defenders. The pilots were bombing blind and had to shorten their attack for fear of hitting their own men.

As the raiding fleet slipped up the estuary, searchlights swept the river, and the ships were caught in their beams. A challenge followed. Sending German Morse Code, the raiding party asked for permission to proceed into harbor. For two valuable miles the Germans were bluffed into holding their fire.

Suddenly, when the *Campbeltown* was about six minutes from the great dock, the guns opened up. Streams of tracer bullets, flying horizontally, lashed the fleet from both banks of the river.

At point-blank range the guns raked the ships. The British guns replied, but the gunners were dazzled by the blinding searchlights. The *Campbeltown*, under the command of Lieutenant Commander Beattie, increased her speed as she neared the target, driving straight for the center of the massive gates. Then, with a resounding crash, her bows were buried in a deep rent of torn steel.

It was an amazing feat. After traveling four hundred and fifty miles in the open sea and five through narrow, closely guarded waters, the last two in the face of shattering fire, the *Campbeltown* scored a direct hit, only four minutes behind schedule. Lieutenant Commander Beattie, the gallant Australian captain of the *Campbeltown*, was awarded a V.C. The complete success of the raid was largely due to the unfaltering seamanship and calm action of this one man.

The explosive charge in the *Campbeltown*'s bows had been set to go off with time fuses. At noon the next day, with a thunderous roar, she blew up. The gates were wrecked so thoroughly that the dock was useless to the Germans for the rest of the war. The commandos too had done their work, and the whole dock area was smashed up.

Of the six hundred and thirty men who sailed from Falmouth four days before, less than half came home. The cost was heavy but the prize great.

In August 1942, five months after the St. Nazaire raid, a costly commando attack was made on Dieppe to gain information for the massed invasion of France later on. The Canadian Army provided the main body of attack, which they carried out with ardent courage. By their sacrifice and tragic experience lessons were learned which saved thousands of lives on D day.

By 1943 American shipbuilding was changing the course of the war. The "two-ocean navy" was a fact. Cargo ships and tankers were rolling off the slipways to fill the gaps torn in the fleets by the U-boats. Warships were being launched each week to guard them. Divisions, fully equipped with the finest modern weapons, were safely convoyed across the Atlantic for the "Torch" landing. Millions of tons of supplies flowed into Britain under the protection of the United States Navy. Early in 1944 the D day build-up began, and the Nazis could not stop it.

After the St. Nazaire raid the *Tirpitz* lay low; but the British battle fleet was tied down in sentry duty, watching her. So in the autumn of 1943 the British Navy decided to strike.

Two midget submarines, under the commands of Lieutenants Cameron and Place, were towed across the North Sea to the mouth of the Norwegian fiord where the *Tirpitz* lay. Alone in enemy waters the two midgets threaded their way up fifty miles of narrow fiord. All the channels leading to the *Tirpitz* were vigilantly patrolled, and the submarines had to weave through closely packed mine fields.

The *Tirpitz* lay in an inner fiord, guarded by anti-submarine nets which had to be cut. Both midget submarines crept through the defenses to the long, grey hull of the battleship. They saw clearly that there was no chance of escape when the mission was over. The captains placed their charges against the thickly armored hull. Then they surfaced, and were taken prisoner.

The effect of the explosions was staggering. The ship rose high in the water, leaping like a wounded shark, and then settled slowly with a bad list. The midget submarines triumphed in their mission, for the *Tirpitz* was out of action.

The Germans worked hard to repair the damage. For more than a year engineers struggled to make the ship seaworthy, while the R.A.F. kept a close watch on their progress.

In October 1944 the *Tirpitz* moved one stage nearer Germany. Then the R.A.F. got to work, flying in through a deadly clatter of flak, pressing home their attacks. After this the *Tirpitz* was given no rest. In the first attack she was damaged, and in November 1944 she was sunk by a force of twenty-nine Lancasters. As three twelve-thousand-pound bombs found their mark the great battleship heeled over at her moorings, capsized and sank.

The ship that had been such a source of pride to

Hitler and such a source of anxiety to the Allies had foundered without ever firing a shot in battle.

At the cost of cruel losses in ships and men the Nazi stranglehold on Britain had been broken. American shipyards were launching new craft every day. The U-boat commanders had lost heart and would no longer drive home their attacks. The two great Nazi battleships lay at the bottom of the sea, and the Italian fleet had surrendered. And in the summer of 1944 Hitler lost command of the French ports. The Battle of the Atlantic had been won.

Then, at long last, the British Navy could join the United States Navy in the battle against Japan in the Pacific.

28

The Battle of Burma

FOR FOUR YEARS before Pearl Harbor China had been at war with Japan. Japanese bombers, tanks, and artillery had laid waste Chinese territory and killed her people. There was no industry in China large enough to produce arms to fight the Japanese on equal terms. The United States, Britain, and Russia sent a trickle of supplies; but the main route was the Burma Road, running north from India, and it could not carry all that China needed. Also, after Hitler's triumphs in Europe in 1940 and 1941 Britain and Russia had no arms to spare.

There was one active force helping Generalissimo Chiang Kai-shek, who was head of the Chinese government and Commander in Chief of the armed forces, in his fight against Japan. In 1937 Colonel Claire Chennault retired from the Air Force and went to China to organize the Chinese Air Force. He was an expert in aerial combat, and he had studied Japanese tactics. He trained and organized

243

the battered Chinese air squadrons, but he badly needed American pilots and modern planes.

Chennault tried for years to interest Washington in the urgent needs of China. Finally in 1941 he got permission to form the American Volunteer Group, and the Flying Tigers were born. The men were recruited from American air stations and paid by the Chinese government. They were both adventurous and highly skilled. The Japanese had met their match in the air.

Chennault stationed his squadrons at Kunming, just north of the Burma Road. From there they guarded the road and beat off raids on Chinese territory. In the first week of combat they triumphantly shot down fifty-five Zeros with the loss of five of their own Tomahawks.

After Pearl Harbor, when the Allies were at open war with Japan, the Flying Tigers moved into Burma to protect Rangoon. This was the port for the supplies which passed up the Burma Road, and it was vitally important to the Allies and also to the Japanese.

Japanese raiders came over by day and night. They wrecked the airfields, the docks, and the city. Outnumbered but undaunted, the Flying Tigers knocked the bombers out of the sky. Their own planes were riddled with bullet holes, and each day fewer were fit to fly. They lost many of their pilots, but the remainder fought on with redoubled resolution. They knew that they could beat the Japanese if they could only get more aircraft. But in 1941 the Allies had none to send. When Rangoon fell, the airfields were lost, and the Flying Tigers returned to Kunming.

In the summer of 1941 Chennault was asked to rejoin the Air Force, and he thought it right to accept. The Tigers had accomplished their mission. Some of them rejoined the Air Force, but many stayed to carry on the war with the Chinese.

Even before the fall of Singapore the Japanese had started an invasion of Burma. The prize of India, gleaming in the distance, lured them on. There was little chance of the poorly armed British, Chinese and Indian forces holding Burma; and, worst of all, they were in terrible danger of being trapped and destroyed. The escape of these forces was vital, for they were the only barrier between the advancing Japanese Army and the Indian frontier.

Retreats are dismal and heartbreaking and call for great leadership. Winston Churchill "could not send an army to Burma so he sent a man." General Alexander (who was later to distinguish himself in North Africa) arrived in Rangoon to take on the melancholy task.

The only escape route for the troops and large numbers of civilian refugees was a six hundred mile trek through jungle, over rivers and across mountain ranges. It was a race between the escaping columns and the monsoon rains, which would turn the jungle into a swamp and the rivers into raging torrents.

The Japanese troops were well equipped for jungle campaigns. They carried walkie-talkies and were supplied with concentrated rations, which kept up their strength; and they knew all the time that there was a stream of reinforcements in their rear.

The Burma Army won the race. Their route was littered with corpses and abandoned vehicles, but on May 17, 1942, two days before the rains broke, they reached the Indian frontier, where they turned to face the enemy. But the British forces were in a bad way. They had lost their equipment and had no air support; and the legend had grown that the Japanese were invincible in the jungle.

As the Japanese troops advanced they cut the Burma Road, and China was isolated, since this was the only land route linking her with the Western Allies. The Americans flew a shuttle service from India over the foothills of the Himalayas, a journey which the pilots called "going over the Hump." It was an expensive way of sending supplies but it kept China in the war. On the return flight they brought back Chinese troops to serve under General Joseph Stilwell. It was an ambitious and highly successful mass troop movement. Thirteen thousand men traveled west over the Hump, without a single casualty.

In 1943 the outlook on the Burma front improved.

American Dakotas and British Spitfires flew in, and the Japanese mastery of the air waned. General Slim arrived to take command of the British Fourteenth Army and General Stilwell's Chinese divisions were being trained in India for jungle fighting. "Vinegar Joe" was one of the great characters of the war. Sixty-five years old, tough and untiring, he drove himself and his men relentlessly. He believed that if Chinese troops were properly trained and equipped they could beat the Japanese. He served in the United States Army with a special appointment to Chiang Kai-shek.

In December Vinegar Joe set out from Ledo, on the Burma-India frontier. He had two aims: one was to push back the Japanese, and the other to build a road which would reopen the way to China. Eighty thousand black, brown, yellow, and white men toiled in the broiling heat, and as Stilwell advanced the road unrolled. Through steaming jungle, over mountain ranges and across rivers, by a herculean effort, it kept pace with the army.

In the spring of 1944 the Fourteenth Army was advancing on the central front in Burma against savage Japanese resistance. The Allies had won the mastery of the air, but the Japanese forces were thick on the ground. At this time, when the Allied armies in Europe were fighting in Italy and massing their forces for the Normandy landing, Burma was at the thin end of the supply line. In March the Japanese forces in Burma launched a violent attack. They had prepared for a long time to sever the thin British lines, outflank the Fourteenth Army and cross into India.

The little hill station of Kohima lies on the Indian frontier, on a narrow saddle five thousand feet above the plains, and there the Japanese forces were held by a tiny force of British soldiers. For fifty days and fifty nights they clung to the pass. In the charred ruins of the little town everyone who could hold a gun confronted the enemy. Kohima was the stand that saved India.

Farther along the India-Burma border, on the Imphal plateau, the Japanese spearhead encircled sixty thousand men of the Fourteenth Army who, supplied only from the air, fought off the enemy attacks.

The Japanese Imperial Command staked everything on this battle. The troops were told that victory in Asia depended on Imphal, and they fought with boundless fury.

Then, on June 22, the Japanese front at Imphal collapsed. Reinforcements streamed through to relieve the British garrison. Fifty thousand Japanese lay dead on the field of battle, and the road to Kohima and the plains was opened.

While the armies were engaged on the long front, two guerrilla forces were causing havoc behind the enemy lines. A secret O.S.S. unit, Merrill's Marauders, named after its leader, worked with a fierce native tribe, the Kachins. They recruited the Kachin warriors, who were born fighters, armed them with modern weapons and directed their raids on Japanese depots and communications.

The other guerrilla force, Wingate's Chindits, was made up of British soldiers, rigorously trained for jungle warfare. They were parachuted in with arms and explosives and supplied by air, so that they could live in the jungle for weeks on end to accomplish some special mission.

Along the Arakan coast in western Burma, troops of the Fourteenth Army pressed on to join a British sea-borne landing at Rangoon. In the sweltering Arakan country it can rain as much in one week during the monsoon season as in New York during a whole year. Always the coming of the monsoon hung over the Burma fighting. When the rains broke the jungle was turned into a stifling swamp where men, mules and vehicles were sucked into the quagmire.

Suddenly the British units near Rangoon discovered that the Japanese had pulled out; they had slipped away in the night and were steadily retreating. Then, at last, in December 1944, after a year of continuous fighting, the Fourteenth Army swung north and joined up with General Stilwell's divisions. With magnificent dash, "Vinegar Joe's" troops had captured the junction and airfield of Myitkyina. He had proved the quality of his Chinese divisions. Together the Allied armies broke out into the plains of Mandalay. Finally, Chiang Kai-shek's armies swept down from China, and the Burma Road was open again.

The Battle of Burma had been won. Pitted against the Japanese, the jungle, the monsoon and a constant shortage of supplies, the Allied forces had gained a great victory. King George VI ordered a special medal to be struck, the Burma Star, for the men who had fought this battle.

29

Island Conquests

THE UNITED STATES had borne almost the whole weight of the war against Japan in the Pacific. As early as the summer of 1942, when America was still short of warships, the victories of the Coral Sea and Midway had abruptly checked the headlong Japanese advance; but there was still a long way to go.

After the defeat in the Philippine Islands in 1942, General MacArthur moved his headquarters to Australia. From there he directed operations in the South Pacific, while Admiral Nimitz, from Pearl Harbor, commanded the forces in the north.

The Japanese had to be driven from the high seas and from the far-flung chain of Pacific islands. Each conquest had to be wrung from an enemy to whom death meant nothing; it was the grimmest form of warfare. Even after their defeat in the Coral Sea the Japanese still hoped to gain a stranglehold on Australia and drive her out of the war.

The little tropical island of Guadalcanal, in the Solomons, northeast of Australia, marked the southernmost tip of the Japanese advance, and in August 1942 a force of United States Marines was landed there to recapture the island.

Swift enemy attack forced the naval ships supporting the landing to withdraw, leaving the Marines, with scanty supplies, to face the enemy as best they could. From the first they were beset with difficulties, for the landing craft were wrecked on the coral reefs off the beaches. The men waded ashore and set up a little area of defense, encircled by a violently active enemy.

From that day, for the next six months, the fighting raged mercilessly on, around and over Guadalcanal. Large Japanese naval forces converged on the island and were beaten off by the Navy with heavy losses to both sides. Eventually, by brilliant strategy, an entire Japanese troop convoy was wiped out, and the pressure dwindled.

The Marines fought hunger, fatigue, and disease as well as the enemy. In the end the Battle of Guadalcanal was won by a slim margin of sheer courage.

One by one the Solomon Islands were wrested from the Japanese. Soon it became clear that they had failed to foresee the vast productive might of the United States. During the Battle of Guadalcanal the Navy had only three aircraft carriers in the Pacific; yet a year later they had fifty, and at the end of the war more than a hundred. And they also had men of skill and valor to man them.

A new and stirring figure had appeared on the scene. Lieutenant Colonel Fordyce Carlson had been convinced for many years that Japan would attack in the Pacific. He had resigned from the Marines to study guerrilla warfare, and he had tried to warn the United States command of the approaching danger.

After Pearl Harbor Carlson returned to the Marines to form a select force of guerrilla fighters. When he called for volunteers he got seven thousand and took one thousand. He chose his men not for their physical fitness but for their determination. They had to know precisely what they were fighting for, and be ready to die for it.

The training was extremely hard. They marched forty miles a day with full packs, learned the ways of the jungle and to kill swiftly and silently. In August 1942 Carlson's Raiders landed on Makin Island in the Gilbert group, to divert Japanese attention from the invasion of Guadalcanal. They smashed the radio station, burned the stores and gasoline and killed every Japanese. Later, on Guadalcanal, the raiders filtered through the enemy lines and, using guerrilla tactics, beat them at their own form of warfare.

Famed for their discipline, their skill, and their fearlessness, Carlson's Raiders became a terror to the Japanese.

While the Marines fought it out on Guadalcanal, General MacArthur also attacked in New Guinea. In a series of leapfrog landings and airborne assaults, the Japanese strong points were surrounded and mopped up. Over its thousand-mile length the island is split by a great spine of mountains covered with jungle forest. The coastal areas are dense with steaming tropical vegetation in which no roads exist. It was a long and arduous campaign fought by Americans and Australians in country where the losses from disease matched those inflicted by the enemy.

By the end of the two years that it took to conquer New Guinea, the endurance and gallantry of the Allied troops had been pushed to the limit.

As the last Japanese resistance on New Guinea faded out, American land, sea, and air forces began to probe the chain of islands that runs northward toward Japan. They developed a system of assault which began with heavy attacks from carrier-based aircraft, followed by withering bombardment from the sea and finally a landing.

The islands were supremely important to the Japanese defense, and they fought fiercely to hold them; for each one was an ocean guard protecting Japan.

From the beginning of the war in the Far East the Japanese had their eyes on the Aleutian Islands in the northern Pacific. The Aleutians stretch in a long arc from the southern tip of Alaska to the Bering Sea. They are American territory, bought from Russia in 1867. In a war these islands have great strategic value, for they could form a springboard for an enemy attack on North America.

In May 1942 the Japanese moved into the Aleutians, capturing the islands of Attu and Kiska, where they easily overpowered the small garrisons manning the weather stations.

The weather around Alaska and the Aleutians is as bad as any in the world. Fog and snow shroud the landscape for most of the year, and driving blizzards sweep through the treacherous channels. Magnetic ore in the rocks sends instruments crazy and makes guesswork of navigation.

The North Pacific Fleet assembled its rather meager forces under Admiral Kinkaid, who had been sent from the South Pacific for the uninviting task of reconquering the Aleutians. In December 1942 an airfield was established on the island of Amchitka, without much opposition.

By the following May a landing force had been collected for the next hop in the Aleutians, the island of Attu at the eastern end, two hundred and fifty miles from Amchitka. Attu was known to be well fortified. As the fleet set out, fog closed down and smothered every landmark. For seven days without a break in the clouds, the fleet groped its way to Attu. It was a triumph of navigation that the task force made a perfect landfall.

Deceived by the weather, the Japanese were taken by surprise. The commander of the island, Colonel Yamazaki, had relaxed his vigilance. The first landing parties crept ashore unopposed. Then the defense sprang into action, and for twenty days, through valleys deep in icy slush, up cliffs crowned with fortifications and over heights raked by Japanese fire, the combat troops inched their way across the island.

The defense of Attu ended in a suicide charge. Screaming, flinging grenades, and slashing with knives and bayonets in disorganized frenzy, the remnants of the Japanese forces flung themselves at the American lines. In the gruesome battle that followed, only twenty-nine of the twenty-three hundred Japanese on Attu were taken alive.

The United States forces wearily prepared for the next onslaught on the neighboring island of Kiska. When they reached the beaches they discovered that the enemy had learned the lesson of Attu and had fled. The reconquest of the Aleutians was complete.

In the summer of 1944 the fleet attacked the Marshall Islands, and then the Marianas. The Japanese fleet was still short of carriers after its losses at Midway, and they did not want to fight; but they dared not allow the Americans to go unchallenged. In a battle between carrier aircraft the Japanese fleet was defeated and fled while the pursuing Americans sank three carriers and a battleship.

The fortified Mariana Islands of Truk, Saipan, Guam, and Tinian were captured by the Americans, who had by this time traveled halfway from Guadalcanal to Tokyo. It was a rude shock for the Japanese Imperial Command.

As United States forces edged northward, air

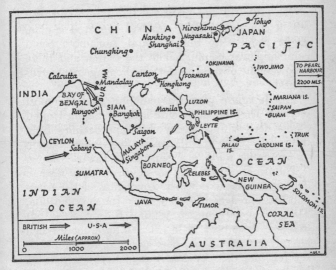

The Allies approach Japan

bases were established and aircraft moved in for the final assault. Bombers were beginning to attack, with increasing strength, cities in Japan itself.

In October 1944 General MacArthur was ready to keep his promise and stage a landing in the Philippines. He wanted to avenge the defeat of 1942 at Bataan and Corregidor, to establish an air base for operations against Japan, and to bring the Japanese fleet to battle. Troops prepared to land on Leyte Island, in the middle of the Philippine group.

The Japanese were afraid of this attack, and they saw it coming, so they also had prepared a plan. Every single ship that Admiral Yamamoto could command was committed to the battle, and there followed one of the greatest naval engagements ever fought.

The Japanese plan was cunning, and it almost worked. They hoped to lure away the main United States fleet with a decoy fleet approaching from the north, while two Japanese fleets would steam up from the south and smash the Leyte landing.

The American landing force, escorted by a small fleet under Admiral Kinkaid, veterans of the Aleutian battle, reached Leyte without much opposition. Their main fleet, under Admiral Halsey, stood out to sea ready to beat off Japanese interference. When aircraft from the decoy fleet attacked, Admiral Halsey fell into the trap and turned north in pursuit, leaving the landing unprotected.

Steaming up from the south with the main Japanese fleet, Admiral Kurita was discovered by American airmen and heavily attacked, losing a battleship and two cruisers. He decided to retreat. At the same time a smaller Japanese fleet attacked the landing and was almost wiped out by Admiral Kinkaid.

Then Kurita turned back to Leyte to fulfill the original plan, for he still had ships that could fight. He fell on Admiral Kinkaid's fleet, catching them when they were exhausted after their recent victory. Outgunned and outnumbered, Kinkaid's fleet was overpowered. Yet deliverance came in an unexpected way: for unknown reasons Kurita turned tail and left the battle at the critical moment when victory was almost in his hands.

In response to Kinkaid's urgent signals Admiral Halsey raced south; but he left enough ships behind to put an end to the decoy fleet, and not a single Japanese carrier survived. Arriving in Leyte Gulf when the battle was over, Admiral Halsey sent ships off in pursuit of Kurita. Fresh and ready for action they tracked down the retreating Japanese fleet and finished it off.

So the Japanese plan ended in total failure, with a loss of three battleships, four aircraft carriers, ten heavy cruisers, nine destroyers, and a submarine, against the American loss of three carriers, three destroyers, and a submarine.

The victory of Leyte Gulf was decisive. The Philippine Islands were reconquered, and the United States regained the mastery of the Pacific Ocean.

At Leyte, Japanese suicide planes, the kamikazis, had appeared in battle for the first time. Each was manned by a single fanatical pilot, a volunteer anxious to die for his Emperor. Packed with high explosive, the kamikazis screamed down on the American ships and did great damage. But, like Hitler's secret weapons in Europe, they were a measure of despair and could not change the course of war.

Later the Allies captured Japanese suicide boats — tiny motorboats carrying a depth charge and designed to ram warships. The man who operated a suicide boat was promised double promotion at the end of his task, but as there was an interval of only five seconds between the impact and the explosion few of them lived to apply for the prize.

The next dangerous destination was the important island base of Iwo Jima, some seven hundred miles from Tokyo. It was a foothold that the Japanese could ill afford to lose, and they had fortified it with everything they could cram in.

Iwo Jima is a tiny barren speck on the Pacific Ocean. Formed of grey volcanic rock, it is only five miles long and two and a half miles across at its widest point. The island has two airfields.

The island presented a forbidding appearance to the invading forces, for nothing had taken root on the bare lava ridges. The flat beaches offered no shred of cover, and heavy batteries commanded every yard of the coastline.

Lieutenant General Kuribayashi commanded the defending troops on Iwo Jima and Lieutenant General H. M. ("Howling Mad") Smith the attacking forces. Admiral Spruance, of Midway renown, was in charge of the vast, complicated concentration of shipping. The grim task of capturing Iwo Jima fell to three divisions of United States Marines.

Carrier-based aircraft hammered the airfields, and ships shelled the fortifications around the landing beaches. Then at early dawn on February 19 the landing began. The floating tanks led the way, followed by wave after wave of Marines. As they reached the shallows they were mowed down by murderous fire. A terrible price was paid to gain the first foothold. The men crouched in the bullet-swept sand while the tanks lumbered up the beaches, plowing through the soft volcanic ash, to attack the gun posts.

By nightfall thirty thousand men had landed, but the shore was a junkyard of damaged landing craft and tanks.

The old volcano of Surabachi towered over the beaches, tunneled with fortifications. All over the island the rocky terraces had been studded with mortar emplacements and machine-gun caves. Neither air bombardment nor shelling could pry the Japanese out of their holes, and tanks could not scale the overhanging ledges; so all the strong points had to be taken by direct assault. They did not fall until every Japanese soldier had been killed.

After four days of wild bayonet charges and hand-to-hand fighting Surabachi was captured by the Marines, and the Stars and Stripes were raised on the summit. The struggle had been so bitter and the triumph so dearly gained that the photograph of the planting of the flag on Surabachi came to symbolize for the American people the supreme heroism of the Marines. In Washington a statue of the flag-raising stands as an official Marine memorial so that this heroism will never be forgotten.

But the battle was not yet over. The Marines moved on to attack the airfields, where every yard of pitted ground cost hundreds of lives.

In a month of barbarous fighting the few Japanese troops who survived were driven across the island to the sea. They made their last stand on the beaches, fighting to the end. General Kuribayashi was killed in battle, and of his army of twenty-three thousand men only two hundred and twelve surrendered.

American forces too paid a bitter price: twenty-two thousand Marines and Navy men were killed and wounded to capture this eight square miles of barren rock.

Even then the Allies were hundreds of miles from the unconquered mainland of Japan. There was more heartbreaking fighting ahead. But far away in Europe victory against Germany was near, for by now, March 1945, a year of great events had seen the Nazis rolled back into their own country.

30

D Day

THE VICTORIOUS CAMPAIGN in Europe began in the map rooms of the Allied generals during the winter of 1943–44. The climax of the war was drawing very close, for Allied strength was mounting fast and Hitler had been thrown on the defensive everywhere, even in Berlin.

Churchill, Roosevelt and Stalin — the Big Three — met for the first time. From their widely separated countries they flew to Teheran, the capital of Iran, to plan the last stage in Nazi defeat. They fixed the landing in France for the following spring, determined that the long years of waiting were to end in a knockout blow.

In Western Europe the R.A.F. and the United States Air Force started to soften up the German defenses, preparing for the landing with systematic skill. All along the French coast they wrecked radar stations and blasted the Luftwaffe on its airfields. Allied fighters flew thousands of sorties, and took on the Germans whenever they could bring them to battle; it was clear that the Luftwaffe pilots were not as keen to fight as they had been in 1940.

American bombers tore up the French railroads to prevent the Germans from bringing up supplies and tackled the bridges in courageous low-level attacks. Soon there was hardly a bridge left in northern France strong enough to carry a Panzer division.

The invasion was carefully planned to the last detail, day by day and hour by hour, and fully rehearsed by Allied soldiers, sailors, and airmen long before the Supreme Commander, General Eisenhower, had decided what the date should be. So, while the teams were training, the invasion date was called "D" or "D day"; the day which would follow it was called "D plus one," the next day "D plus two" and so on. In this way the most exact plans could be made in advance.

D day was finally set for June 5, and the beaches east of the Cherbourg peninsula in Normandy were selected for the landing. In Britain a mighty force was assembled — two million men and a massive stock of every kind of weapon. They flowed in from America by sea and by air.

General Eisenhower arrived from Italy to take command of Supreme Headquarters Allied Expeditionary Force, the initials forming the name SHAEF, soon to become so famous. Under him were the finest commanders that could be found — General Omar Bradley, whom Ike had picked out and promoted for this job, General Montgomery, and the

Canadian General Crerar. Air Chief Marshal Sir Leigh Mallory was Air Commander in Chief, and Admiral Sir Bertrand Ramsey, of Dunkirk fame, commanded the vast invasion fleet.

It was agreed that General Montgomery should command all the land forces in Normandy and that later Generals Bradley, Patton, Joe Collins, and Courtenay Hodges should lead their own armies in the advance through France while Monty commanded the British and Canadian Twenty-first Army Group.

Harbors are vital to the landing of a modern army, and it was obvious that the Germans would destroy the ports rather than let them fall into Allied hands. So it was decided that the armies would have to take their harbors with them — they must be built in Britain and towed over. It sounded like a fairy tale, but it came true.

The "mulberry" harbors came into being. They were built from huge hollow concrete blocks, towed over and sunk end to end to form a pier. Cranes and winches for unloading were added, and a port grew up overnight. The American and British Armies each had a "mulberry."

"Pluto" was invented, the name coming from "pipe line under the ocean." It was a long flexible pipe, designed to run under the sea from England to Normandy. Thousands of gallons of fuel could be pumped through it every day to keep the Allied armies on the move.

The hour of the landing was supremely important. In summer the nights are short and every minute precious. A rising tide was essential, otherwise the landing craft would be stranded on the beaches, easy prey for enemy guns.

The weather was a matter of grave concern, since even the most careful planners could not control it and a stormy sea would be the best ally that Hitler could have. Every other detail and possibility of disaster was examined by the experts. Photographs were taken which showed an ominous array of obstacles planted off the beaches.

Even the surface of the beaches was studied for patches of clay or mud that might clog the machines. Allied submarines stood off the French coast at night while men swam ashore and brought back samples.

Southern England became one vast camp, teeming with men and piled high with materials of war. The area was shut off from the rest of the country. People in Britain watched with awe the stream of tanks, guns, trucks, and armored bulldozers, nose to tail, pouring down to the south coast. They got used to the clank and rumble of heavy wheels all day and through the night.

Tension ran high. Everyone knew that D day was at hand. Only a chosen few knew precisely when or where the landing would take place.

The commanders toured the units and talked to men of all ranks, so that the troops got to know their leaders and had faith in them. On the eve of the great battle, morale was high.

The enemy could not fail to know that the English harbors were jammed with shipping, and great pains were taken to deceive the Germans with mock preparations for a landing near Calais. Dummy ships were put where the enemy could see them. Sham gliders made of plywood were stacked on the airfields near Dover, and rubber tanks were blown up to represent an armored division. This trick was a great success, and for weeks valuable Nazi divisions guarded the Channel ports against an invasion that never came.

On May 15 a full-scale conference was held in Montgomery's headquarters in London with all the Commanders in Chief present, so that the final plans could be rounded off. Both King George VI and Winston Churchill attended.

You will see on the diagram how the forces were disposed: Americans landing on the western beaches nearest Cherbourg, with the British and Canadians on their left. American and British airborne landings were to flank each army.

Deep fear was felt for the airborne landings, particularly the American. They were vital to the seizing of strategic points for the protection of the troops on the beaches in the first few hours; but the Normandy country was cut up into small fields with high hedges and wide ditches, fatal to gliders. General Eisenhower had to make the grave decision of sending ten thousand of his best troops, the pick of his army, perhaps to die on the first day of battle.

Just before D day SHAEF moved to Portsmouth,

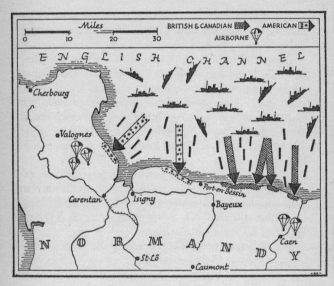

D day landing

in the south of England. The assault troops were briefed and ready. General Eisenhower said in his book *Crusade in Europe*, "The whole mighty host was tense as a coiled spring."

The weather experts worked out the prospects, but their meeting with the Commanders in Chief at 4 A.M. on June 4, the day before D day, was held in heavy gloom. High winds and stormy seas were predicted: already clouds tore across the sky, and breakers swept in on the Normandy beaches. The landing was postponed, and for twenty-four hours the armies waited in stark suspense.

General Eisenhower wrote that by the morning of June 5 the camp was "shaking and shuddering under a wind of almost hurricane violence and the rain traveled in horizontal streaks." If D day had not been put off, disaster would have overwhelmed the landing forces. Small boats and landing craft could not have lived in the surf, and the air forces would have been grounded.

Then suddenly the weathermen foretold an improvement — not a long one, but a lull in the storm. The Supreme Commander took the decision: they would attack the next morning, June 6. The orders were flashed to the waiting host.

Under gray skies the great armada set out. All around the south coast of England the harbors released their long train of shipping, heading south to Normandy. The airborne troops took off a few hours later, under cover of darkness, to land just ahead of the beach forces.

At SHAEF the Commander in Chief waited. After a few hours a trickle of news started, and the first reports were good. The airborne landings had been made without the dreaded loss. The invasion fleet had been shielded by low clouds and the Germans taken by surprise — most of their radar stations had been put out of action by pre-D day bombing. The German coastal guards had relaxed their vigilance because of the storm. Rommel, who was in command of the defending army, had gone to Germany to see Hitler.

The first waves of troops landed on the beaches and made contact with their airborne units. Soon resistance stiffened. The worst fighting developed on the American left flank next to the British sector. By daylight the Germans were alerted all along the coast, and guns swept the beaches.

Nevertheless the landings and build-up went on although casualties on the beaches and in the landing craft were heavy. If their boats were wrecked the men waded ashore through the waves, while tanks and trucks rumbled up the beaches. Gradually the defenders were driven from their gun posts, and a continuous front of about fifty miles was forged by the Allied armies.

General Eisenhower broadcast to the enslaved people of Europe, telling them that liberation was at hand.

The Allied strategy had two aims: first, to establish a beachhead and second, to expand it. The British and Canadian troops were to engage the main German strength round Caen, while the Americans captured Cherbourg and then broke out southward. Caen was the hinge of the Nazi line, and they fought furiously to hold it. Once more Montgomery and Rommel were locked in battle.

The "mulberries" served well. Over five thousand ships and landing craft took part in the landing. When Churchill visited the beaches a week after D day he steamed in through what he described as "a city of ships." "Pluto" worked overtime.

The Allied air forces were supreme, covering the beaches with an air umbrella. After a week, air strips were laid down, and the fighters moved in.

In Germany Hitler had pinned the people's faith to his "miracle weapons." After each setback and as an answer to Allied bombing the Nazi news and radio predicted a miraculous salvation. Goebbels said that when the right time came the Führer would unleash the weapons, so that Britain would crumble in ruins and all Germany's enemies would be struck down.

The Allied leaders were well aware that this was not all talk, for the aerial photographs had shown curious buildings on the French coast which did not fit into any known form of warfare. These were the launching sites for the secret weapons, and both the American Eighth Air Force and the R.A.F. had bombed them hard.

On June 13, just one week after D day, the first "flying bomb" hit England. During the next two and a half months many others followed. Aimed at London, they came over day and night, in all weathers, at irregular intervals, so that people never felt safe.

The new weapons came to be known as V-bombs. They were small, pilotless aircraft, carrying a large load of high explosive, and they flew on a course set by internal mechanism. When the course was complete the engine stopped, and the flying bomb fell to earth with a deadly explosion.

People grew wise, listening carefully for the horrible hum of the flying-bomb engine, and when it stopped they dived for cover. They called the bombs "doodle bugs" and "buzz bombs." They did not reduce Britain to ruins, nor did they win the war for Hitler, but they killed people and added to the hardship at a time when the nation was very tired of war.

Antiaircraft guns were moved to the coast, a balloon barrage went up around London and fighters took off and shot the flying bombs down over the sea. But some still got through, and it was only when the launching sites were captured by the Allies that the people in Britain could relax.

Then a new terror started: bombs which were called V2s to distinguish them from the buzz bombs. They were high-speed rockets, launched in Holland, which rose fifty miles into the air traveling at nearly four thousand miles an hour. They landed in or near London, and there was no warning of their arrival. The first sign was a deafening explosion, followed by the high whine of their passage through the air, since they traveled faster than sound. Fortunately for the long-suffering Londoners Hitler could not produce many V2s. Their manufacture and launching was a complicated process, made much more difficult by Allied bombing.

31

Victory Rolls On

MEANWHILE, IN NORMANDY, the worst June storm in forty years broke over the beachhead, so that neither men nor materials could be landed for three days. The mulberries broke loose and were driven against the anchored shipping, causing chaos. When the storm ended the engineers set to work to repair the damage, and the build-up continued; but the Germans had used the interval to strengthen their defenses.

Cherbourg fell to the Americans on June 26, after nearly three weeks' siege. General Collins had kept to the Commander in Chief's post-D day schedule and lived up to his own nickname of "Lightning Joe" by the speed and pressure of his assault. The Germans reduced the port to ruins before they surrendered.

On July 25 General Patton, leading the American Third Army, broke out of the peninsula. With dash and shrewd mobile tactics he swept south through

Brittany, helped everywhere by the Resistance fighters, who had been secretly armed by the Allies and were waiting for this moment.

In this month American forces in Europe outnumbered the British for the first time, and their numbers rose rapidly. General Montgomery still commanded all the land forces, but General Bradley was soon to take over the American armies.

On July 17 Rommel was seriously wounded by air attack, and while he was in the hospital an attempt was made on Hitler's life. As the Führer presided at a conference Colonel von Stauffenburg, an officer who had distinguished himself in the Afrika Korps, placed a brief case, containing a time bomb, against the leg of the table where Hitler sat and then left the room. A few minutes later the bomb exploded, but although officers all round him were killed, Hitler escaped with slight injuries. He had been protected by the heavy top of the table and the thin walls of the room, which had let out the blast.

Many high-ranking German officers had shared in the plot. Knowing that Germany was beaten they wanted to get rid of Hitler before he dragged the nation down to utter ruin. Rommel was one of them.

Hitler's revenge was merciless. Hundreds of men, many of them innocent, were tortured and shot. Rommel chose suicide rather than public execution and killed himself.

In the Caen area the British and Canadians had

been holding fast in the face of massed attacks by German armored divisions. At the end of June formations of Allied heavy bombers went in ahead of the Twenty-first Army Group and leveled Caen to the ground. Following closely on the bombardment the British and Canadian forces attacked and, fighting their way through the piles of debris, captured the ruined town. The hinge of the German line was bent.

Canadian forces under General Crerar pressed on from Caen, down the road to Falaise. Everywhere they found total devastation where the air forces had attacked behind the German lines. They passed through the tragic remains of villages without a single house standing; the inhabitants had fled and were hiding in the woods.

Hitler's generals had been urging him to withdraw the German armies to save them from disaster. The Führer not only refused to give a yard but ordered five Panzer divisions to attack and cut off General Patton and his Third Army in Brittany.

The German thrust was held with tremendous gallantry at its critical point by a single United States division. When Allied help came the Germans were driven back in confusion; General Patton swung up sharply from Brittany, and the British forces closed in from the north. The German spearhead was cut off and trapped in a bulging pocket. The Panzer divisions were seasoned troops, and they fought to break out with savage determination.

The job of sewing up the pocket was given to the

Canadians, and in this engagement Major Currie won the first Canadian V.C. in northwest Europe. With a force of a hundred and seventy-five men he led an attack on the little village of St. Lambert, blocked the German escape and held them "in the bag" against violent counterattacks until reinforcements arrived. Then the Panzer army was sealed in, and the Allied air forces got to work.

Hundreds of bombers, diving, twisting and diving again, pounded the surging crowd of trapped men and vehicles. On the verges the Allies brought their guns to bear on the tangled ranks of the broken army. In the massed turmoil almost everything was destroyed, and when the gunfire died down a dead army lay in the Falaise pocket.

The tattered remnants of the German armies fled in confusion from this area with the Allies at their heels, while the Allied air forces constantly harassed the retreating columns. They had already cut the bridges and railroads on the escape route. The dusty French roads were stained with a litter of dead Nazis and smashed vehicles.

Once the hard-fought battles in Normandy had been won the Allied armies raced across France. The Americans started the Red Ball Express, chains of trucks chasing the armies, supplying them with food, medical stores and ammunition. An oil pipeline was laid, running abreast of the fighting front, to keep the huge mechanical force in action — an outstanding feat of organization.

General Eisenhower determined not to risk the destruction of Paris by frontal attack. American and French divisions steadily surrounded the city, while inside Paris French patriots rose against the Nazis. They sent officers through the Allies' lines to establish contact with the advancing armies. Free French units were given the honor of liberating their capital. Under Colonel Billotte, son of the general killed in 1940, an armored column advanced into the center of Paris and accepted the surrender of the German commander.

On August 25, 1944, General de Gaulle and General Leclerc marched down the Champs Élysées amid scenes of passionate rejoicing. In Notre Dame Cathedral the liberation of Paris was solemnly celebrated.

By this time a new invasion had taken place, for on August 14 Allied troops had landed in the south of France against light resistance, swinging northwards to join the advancing armies.

When the Americans turned towards Paris the British Twenty-first Army Group under General Montgomery struck north from Normandy, along the coast. They overran the flying-bomb sites, recaptured Le Havre, Calais, Boulogne and Dunkirk. They stood where the B.E.F. had stood in 1940. Brussels fell on September 3 and Antwerp next day.

As fall came, the Allied armies were closing up to the banks of the Rhine. Belgium and Luxembourg had been set free and the Nazis driven back along the whole front. But the Allied lines of supply were becoming strained, and the armies were living from hand to mouth with nothing to spare; the Red Ball Express had reached its limit.

On the Belgian-Dutch frontier the British Army had come to a standstill. The path was blocked by three rivers, the Meuse, the Waal, and the Lower Rhine, each river being spanned by a great bridge closely guarded by strong German forces. Montgomery, now a Field Marshal, formed a bold plan to capture the bridges by airborne assault, making a giant leapfrog into Germany.

The two bridges nearest the British lines, one at Eindhoven and the other at Nijmegen, were to be taken by American airborne units and the farthest bridge at Arnhem by the British First Airborne Division under General Urquhart. The dangers of the Arnhem force were bound to be very great. Owing to shortage of aircraft the men had to be dropped on three successive days, so the first landing would be perilously small.

On September 17 the airborne units took off from England. At Eindhoven and Nijmegen Americans captured the bridges after hard fighting. At Arnhem, on the first day, United States Dakotas skillfully dropped three British parachute battalions and landed two hundred and ninety-seven gliders. The men were put down on high ground outside the town, and they formed parties and moved into Arnhem to capture the bridge. But almost at once active resistance flared up; the airborne forces had to fight their way from house to house and street to street, helped by Dutch patriots but strongly opposed by the German forces stationed in the town.

Men of the Second Parachute Battalion under Colonel Frost won a footing on the bridge and prepared to hold the precarious position until reinforcements came. For days they clung to their ground, hoping every hour for help, until in the end they were killed or captured.

The rest of the airborne forces were scattered through the town and the surrounding country. Joined next day by the second landing, but unable to make contact with the Polish units who were dropped on the third day, the men fought their way toward the bridge. Under conditions of intense danger and increasing hardship, tormented by lack of food and water, and short of ammunition, their number shrank daily. Either pinned down on the high ground on Arnhem ridge without protection from constant air attack or hemmed into a small area on the river bank, they hung on desperately, counting on relief from the Nijmegen forces who never got through.

On the eighth day General Urquhart saw that the situation was hopeless and ordered a withdrawal across the river.

The survivors of the airborne division, many carrying wounded comrades, escaped by night in little boats or by swimming the river, and made their weary way to Nijmegen. Of the ten thousand men who had landed at Arnhem, just over two thousand reached the British lines. Of the gallant Second Parachute Battalion of seven hundred men, under twenty came back that day.

The full plan had failed, but the advance to the Nijmegen bridge by American units was firmly held. Gained at bitter cost, it formed the springboard from which the Allied armies leaped into Germany a few months later.

Once the Belgian port of Antwerp was opened to the Allies supplies poured in, and preparations for the attack on Germany began. After the crushing blows which had struck the German Army from all sides and the battering which the Allied bombers had given Germany, it seemed unlikely that the Nazis could do more than defend their own frontiers.

But in December the Allied armies suffered a sharp reverse.

Once more Hitler had refused to accept defeat. He was ill and badly shaken after the attempt on his life in July. Living in a concrete dugout, closely guarded by the Gestapo, he was shut off from the world. He was far above ordinary events and still dreamed of a magic revival of Nazi power.

In December he summoned his commanders from the Western Front and unfolded his plans. In an astonishing recovery after the defeats in France, twenty-four German divisions, including ten Panzers, had been scraped together. Hitler ordered this force to attack through the Ardennes, sever the Allied armies, sweep north to capture Brussels and Antwerp and repeat his dramatic triumph of 1940.

It was a fantastic plan, but Hitler still commanded some fanatically faithful Nazis who were eager to carry it out.

On December 10, led by General Rundstedt, who had commanded the victorious attack in 1940, the Germans struck. The American First Army, which was thinly spread over the Ardennes front, was taken completely by surprise. On the first day of the attack the Panzers punched two deep holes in the American lines. The situation was chaotic — the American front was split, the command divided and communications upset. German commando units, disguised in American uniforms, driving captured tanks and speaking good "American," added to the confusion. At one important crossroad a Nazi dressed as a United States sergeant tangled up the traffic.

The Allied air forces were grounded by fog, and the first snow of the winter fell over the Ardennes forest.

The American command reacted quickly and regrouped its forces; but there was a critical interval. A magnificent stand by the United States 7th Armored Division at St. Vith halted the headlong dash of the Panzer divisions. Often isolated and without orders, the rank and file of the First Army fought nobly. Morale was high. In the little town of Bastogne airborne troops under the command of General McAuliffe were cut off and surrounded by the surging Panzer army. The story is told that when a command to surrender came through from the Nazi general, Tony McAuliffe gave the one-word reply: "Nuts," and went on fighting. The airborne troops held their small area of defense for days until they were relieved. "Nuts" came into the vocabulary of the people of Bastogne as a gesture of defiance and has endured to this day.

By the time reserves were thrown into the front the Germans had driven a wedge fifty miles west, toward the Meuse. This dangerous salient gave the name "the Battle of the Bulge" to the operation.

Back in the summer of 1944 the Allies had held high hopes of winning the war that year, but by Christmas the hopes were dashed and they were still fighting hard.

By February 1945 the German attack in the Ardennes had lost its sting. The Allies, with General Patton attacking from the south and the British forces from the north, had managed to plug the gap. Losses had been very heavy on both sides, but the Germans had been beaten back from the Meuse, and Brussels and Antwerp were safe.

On January 1, 1945, the Luftwaffe had its last fling. Striking at Allied forward airfields the bombers did a lot of damage, but two hundred German aircraft were lost — more than Hitler could afford. He never tried again.

32

The Last Days of Hitler

THE CURTAIN WAS rising for the last act of the war in Europe. Like great battering rams the Allied armies struck at Germany from every side, and she reeled back under the blows. The wrath which Hitler had kindled against Nazi tyranny had mounted to an irresistible force. All over the world an immense flood of armaments had gained momentum. From the vast industrial resources of America, from the wide reaches of the Commonwealth, from the Russian factories in the Ural Mountains, and from the British Isles an unbroken procession of tanks, guns, aircraft, ships, and ammunition flowed to the war fronts.

On three fronts the Allied armies closed their grip on Germany.

In the south, after the capture of Rome, the American Fifth Army and the British Eighth Army pursued the retreating Germans. The beautiful city of Florence fell almost intact to the Allies, and they crossed the river Arno.

The Nazi General Kesselring had prepared for a withdrawal, having first fortified the natural barrier of the Apennine Mountains running from Pisa to Rimini — the Gothic Line. It was a fine defensive position, stretching across Italy from coast to coast. There the German armies dug in.

In September 1944 the Allied armies attacked the Gothic Line. They stormed the heights and broke through in several places, but they were not strong enough to take advantage of their gains. In the waterlogged valleys, drenched by the autumn rains, the enemy fiercely contested every foot of ground.

The Allied Fifth and Eighth Armies in Italy had fought a disheartening war with unfailing gallantry. They had always been short of men; now they had been stripped again to make up the landing force for the south of France. After each hard-won advance they found their path barred by another mountain range or a new river. Again and again their success fell just short of victory.

Finally, in April 1945, a tremendous air bombardment dislodged the Germans from their mountain strongholds, and their supply lines were battered out of existence. The famous Brenner Pass, where Hitler and Mussolini had met with pomp and ceremony to decide how they would rule Europe, was blocked with debris. Then, at last, the Allied armies streamed through the Gothic Line and routed the enemy.

In the north of Italy the partisans had lain in hiding in the mountains. Now, at a given signal, they

Allied armies close in on Hitler

rose and joined the Allied armies, seizing towns and villages from the Nazi garrisons and hastening the surrender of the big cities.

Mussolini had met his end. On April 25 he tried to escape to Switzerland, disguised in German uniform. A partisan patrol halted the car, recognized the ex-Duce and arrested him. The next day Mussolini was shot by the partisans. His body, with that of other Fascists, was sent to Milan. They were exhibited in the market place on meat hooks, strung up by the feet.

There were few mourners.

On April 29, knowing that the Allies were already at the gates of Berlin, General Vietinghoff, who had just succeeded General Kesselring, signed an unconditional surrender at Field Marshal Alexander's headquarters. The bitter battles in Italy were over. The Italian people, most of whom had hated the war, were freed at last.

In Russia, the crushing defeat of the German Sixth Army at Stalingrad in February 1943 had marked the turning point in the war. Though Hitler drove his armies and his people through years of suffering and slaughter, he never repeated his early triumphs.

In July 1943 the Germans launched the most powerful armored attacks of the whole war. The Russians resisted on an even greater scale, and millions of men and thousands of tanks were locked in a raging, swaying battle. The Red Army fell back and then held fast; the last great Nazi bid for victory had failed, with terrible loss.

The following October the Russians opened an offensive along the whole front. The German armies, though at first they clung to their positions, knew they were due for the agony of another Russian winter. Gradually they were forced back. The Red Army advanced from the Caucasian oil fields to the Donets basin with its coal mines and factories, and on through the rich farmland of the Ukraine.

By the spring of 1944 Marshal Stalin announced in an Order of the Day that the Germans had retreated over a thousand miles. Hitler had forbidden his generals to yield an inch of Russian soil, but the days were past when they could carry out the orders of their Führer.

Marshal Zhukov, hero of the battle which saved Moscow in 1941, was Commander in Chief of the Red Army under Stalin. The Russian losses had been stupendous; no other army could have survived such massacre and pressed on to victory.

On June 22, 1944, two and a half weeks after the Normandy landing and precisely three years from the day that Hitler invaded Russia, Stalin launched his last great offensive. He had mustered five hundred divisions, twenty-two thousand guns, four thousand tanks, and five thousand aircraft. The Germans were outnumbered in men and armor, and with a mighty cannonade the Red Army broke through their lines and fanned out towards the west.

By the end of July the Russian armies had crossed

the Polish frontier and were only ten miles from Warsaw. Within the city the Polish Underground Army rose against the hated Nazi garrison to hasten the liberation of their country. They had secretly stored up food and ammunition and had been waiting to attack with passionate eagerness.

The Germans rushed in troops to suppress the rising, and the Russian armies halted. Stalin refused to drop supplies by air to the Polish patriots or to allow British and American aircraft to land on Soviet airfields. He had clearly shown that he would not allow Poland to be set free by anyone but Communists. He had no interest in humanity, no feeling for the suffering of the Polish people. Communism stood above everything.

For sixty-three agonizing days the half-armed Poles in Warsaw held out, fighting with despairing heroism against every weapon and ruthless atrocity that the Nazis could bring to the battle. The British and American Air Forces made one attempt to supply the patriots from their remote airfields, but it was too late. The German vengeance was complete, and when the Russians finally entered the city it was a scene of desolation.

By the time that victory in Europe was in sight Allied unity was wearing thin. The ties which had bound Russia to the United States and Britain in the time of desperate peril were parting. As the danger of war grew less, the danger of communism showed up, and wide differences of opinion began to divide the Big Three.

Meanwhile, Hitler's other conquests were slipping away. Rumania surrendered to the Red Army. In Yugoslavia, Marshal Tito's forces joined with the Soviet armies to liberate Belgrade. Soviet troops had marched through Finland and entered Norway. The capture of Prague and Vienna was delayed until the following spring, but by February the Red Army had invaded Germany and stood only thirty-five miles from Berlin. The German armies had been ripped to pieces.

On the Western Front, early in 1945, when the Battle of the Bulge was over, the Allies prepared for the final drive. The wide waters of the Rhine flowed before them — a formidable barrier. On the central front General Bradley gathered his forces for the attack. In the north, the British Twenty-first Army Group and in the south, the French First Army stood side by side with the Americans. Still fighting obstinately, the German armies were driven back, and as they retreated across the river they blew up the bridges behind them.

On March 7 an unexpected and decisive stroke of good fortune befell the American armies, when, following closely on the heels of the fleeing Germans, they found the great Ludendorff Bridge at Remagen intact. The Germans had been taken by surprise, for they had meant to destroy the bridge as soon as their own troops had crossed; but they had left it too long. It was a wonderful chance. General Bradley grasped it instantly and flung five divisions across the Rhine. The great west wall of Germany was breached.

The Germans struggled to reverse their failure. In the end the Ludendorff Bridge collapsed under their constant bombing, but by this time American engineers had built pontoon bridges, and the passage was secure.

Hitler changed his Commander in Chief in the west for the third time. In a futile effort to stem the tide of Allied victory he brought Kesselring up from Italy to replace von Rundstedt, but neither of them was able to work miracles.

On March 23, with a mighty airborne landing and a strong force of assault boats, the armies under Montgomery forced a crossing over the Rhine just north of the Ruhr. Winston Churchill had arrived to share the great moment. On the day after the attack he crossed the Rhine in a small boat in the midst of the battle and set foot on German soil.

The northern armies swept around the Ruhr and joined hands with General Bradley's forces, and on April 18 the entire Ruhr garrison surrendered. The industrial heart of Germany had stopped beating.

On April 12 President Roosevelt died. He had steered his country through the perilous years with unfailing faith and courage. It was a tragedy that he did not live to see the final victory, although he knew that, at least in Europe, it was near. Americans all over the world mourned a gallant leader, and in every Allied country the people felt that they had lost a loyal friend and a powerful force in the cause of freedom. Vice-President Harry S. Truman became President and carried on the Grand Alliance.

The Nazi front in the west had collapsed, and the routed German forces gave themselves up in hordes to escape capture by the Russians, whose vengeance they feared more. The Allied armies swept on, liberating their own prisoners as they went.

The stark horror of the concentration camps was revealed. The Allied troops were greeted by throngs of starved and tortured human beings, and medical teams took over the camps to care for the living and bury the dead.

On April 25, American troops joined hands with the Russians, who had encircled Berlin that day.

In January, Hitler had moved his headquarters from the Wolf's Lair in East Prussia to Berlin. Years before, at the height of his power, he had built himself the Chancellery, a majestic and luxurious setting for a supreme dictator, ruler of a great nation. Now it stood in the center of a ruined city, and he lived in a deep concrete bunker in the garden.

After the last attempt on his life Hitler was ill and very frightened, hardly ever going out and eating nothing that was not cooked in his own kitchen for fear of poisoning. He was surrounded by the Gestapo, who searched everyone who came near him for hidden weapons. The bomb explosion had damaged his ear drums, and he had a nervous trembling of one hand. All his vigor had left him, and he moved like an old man. Detached from reality, the Führer continued to send orders to armies that had ceased to exist.

With his enemies closing in on all sides Hitler still ranted about the glorious might of Nazi Germany. Flying into uncontrollable rages at any mention of defeat, he screamed of "weaklings and traitors" who had betrayed him.

It is a remarkable fact that even at the end, when their world was crashing round them, there were people who had faith in Hitler. When there was nothing left but death and destruction, they still felt that he had power to save them.

Hitler had learned nothing. A few days before he died he made a last statement to the German people filled with his old hatred of the Jews. He expressed no shame and no regrets. He had not changed since he lived in the slums of Vienna, but he had dragged the German people down to the lowest depths of disaster.

Though most of the prominent Nazis escaped from Berlin, Hitler decided to stay. He chose Admiral Doenitz, who had commanded the U-boat fleet, as his successor, unable to accept the fact that there was nothing left to succeed to.

Hitler himself did not live to face his judges; he chose the easier way out.

Early in the morning on April 29, when the Russians were only a few blocks from the Chancellery, Hitler married Eva Braun, who had come to join him in the bunker. Next day he had his favorite

Alsatian dog Blondi, destroyed, gave his wife poison and shot himself. Doenitz told the nation that Hitler died fighting at the head of his armies.

Hitler left instructions for his body to be burned. He did not wish to be strung up on a meat hook like Mussolini.

On the following day Goebbels, Hitler's most faithful supporter, killed his wife, his five children and finally himself, in the same bunker.

On May 7 the German Commander in Chief signed an unconditional surrender to the representatives of America, Britain, France and Russia.

The war in Europe was ended. The Nazi system had survived its founder by only one week.

In every country that had fought Hitler people were filled with deep thankfulness and overwhelming relief. Crowds thronged the churches. In Washington they turned to the White House, and in London they waited outside Buckingham Palace to show their loyalty to the King and Queen who had shared their danger and sorrows.

They sought out Winston Churchill. He stood before the people he had served so faithfully and gave them the V-sign. To the crowds in Whitehall he said: "God bless you all. This is your victory! It is the victory of the cause of freedom in every land. In our own history we have never seen a greater day than this."

But though Europe was at peace, the war against Japan still had to be won.

Winston Churchill spoke again to the nation and

the Commonwealth, praising their fortitude. It was just five years since he had become Prime Minister — five years of toil, torment, and triumph. He said: "I told you hard things at the beginning of these last five years; you did not shrink, and I should be unworthy of your confidence and generosity if I did not still cry: Forward, unflinching, unswerving, indomitable, till the whole task is done and the whole world safe and clean."

33

Okinawa

On April 1, 1945, two weeks after the fall of Iwo
Jima, American forces attacked Okinawa in the Ry-
ukyu Islands, only three hundred and fifty miles
south of Japan. By this time small units of the British fleet had joined the Americans in the Pacific.

It was a massive attack; thirteen hundred ships
under the command of Admiral Turner backed up
the landing. The softening-up process, with concentrated bombardment from sea and air, followed the
established pattern. Amphibian tanks, guarded by
gunboats, led the way to the beaches. Marine divisions followed, with units of Army infantry and
more tanks. There was no opposition on the beaches;
an ominous calm reigned. There was not a Japanese
soldier to be seen. By nightfall sixty thousand men
were ashore, and still the enemy lay low. The troops
moved cautiously inland.

For five days there was a curious lull on Okinawa.
Then as the landing forces reached the Japanese

first line of defense, the Shuri line, the storm broke. From strongly fortified positions in the craggy terraces and from hills honeycombed with bombproof caves, the Japanese poured out a cannonade of fire. The Marines found themselves attacking across valleys filled with jumbled masses of boulders and scrub, with the enemy always above them.

At the same time a tornado of destruction hit the fleet. Hundreds of kamikazi and other aircraft roared in from airfields on Okinawa and Japan. The suicide planes hurtled down among the ships. The Japanese threw in everything — their prize battleship, the *Yamato* and nine other warships joined the battle. Admiral Spruance's torpedo bombers attacked boldly through low cloud and rain squalls, and only four battered Japanese ships crawled back to port. The *Yamato* sank with her admiral and many of her crew — and a large part of Japanese hopes.

The Japanese had planned first to wipe out the fleet, leaving the land forces stranded, then to mop them up. General Ushojima commanded a hundred and eleven thousand men in Okinawa ready to carry out the second operation.

The damage to the fleet was formidable but not fatal. Supplies continued to come in, and the land forces under the able command of General Buckner, veteran of many battles, hardened to their task.

For days and weeks the Marine, infantry, and tank divisions strove to pierce the Shuri line. As they stormed each rocky crest, another loomed before them, crammed with Japanese. The names of the battles tells the story. Men fought and died on Bloody Ridge; they battled on and on in a welter of butchery and torment on Tombstone Hill; the Battles of the Crags and Pinnacles were fought cave by cave, a deathly nightmare, with each peak falling in the end only to assault with grenades, bayonets, and knives.

Outstanding valor was universal. A typical act of heroism took place when a company was ordered to seize a heavily defended ridge. As the men charged the slope the Japanese opened fire. Most of the company was forced back, but the leading platoon under T/Sergeant Ernest Schoeff kept on, and with eight of his men he reached the top. From fifty to sixty heavily armed Japanese set on the Americans. Schoeff and his platoon beat off the attack in wild hand-to-hand fighting. When the Japanese withdrew he still did not retreat. He held his post all day in the face of large numbers of the enemy, and during the night he led the five survivors of his platoon back to the company.

On April 29 the Shuri line cracked, and the haggard American troops prepared for the next goal. They withstood a counterattack by General Ushojima's hard-driven divisions. The final Japanese orders read: "Each soldier will kill at least one American devil."

In May the rains started, and the Japanese retired into the ruined town of Shuri. Through sodden valleys and over swollen rivers the American troops forged their way into the outskirts of the town. By the time Shuri fell, it was a waste of splintered rubble.

The enemy air attack went on to the end. The supply of fanatics to man the kamikazis did not fail. Nineteen hundred dived to death at Okinawa. Three thousand other Japanese planes were also destroyed.

Ernie Pyle, America's most popular war correspondent, was killed on Okinawa. He had been wherever there was danger from the blitz on London, through the North African landing and D day to the Pacific battles. His reports had carried the spirit of the GIs to their families at home, and they had all loved him.

The American troops won the battle by stark courage. For eighty days they fought unwaveringly against an enemy who knew neither fear nor mercy. Through the tunneled caves and passages of the limestone heights, over mountains and chasms, through floods and under ceaseless fire, they hunted the enemy. Near the end of the battle, with victory in sight, General Buckner, who had commanded the Marines since the landing, was killed by a Japanese shell.

On June 20 General Ushojima's army collapsed. Weakened by eighty days of slow defeat, the soldiers lost discipline and turned into a milling mob. From Tokyo calls came to the "Blood and Youth Organization" to make a glorious stand, but they were nearly all dead.

The remnants of the defeated army crowded to the water's edge and were called upon to surrender;

but, true to their teaching, most of them held grenades to their stomachs and committed hara-kiri, a last tribute to their Emperor. Over a hundred thousand Japanese died on Okinawa.

General Ushojima made the only possible Japanese atonement for his failure. He and his second-in-command, General Cho, ate a splendid meal; then Ushojima in full field uniform and Cho in a white kimono fell on their swords.

On June 22 the American flag was raised over Okinawa. The strains of "The Star-Spangled Banner" floated out on a quiet Pacific breeze, and the veterans of the long battle stood to attention. Twelve thousand five hundred Americans had laid down their lives on Okinawa for this moment.

34

The Atom Bomb and Final Surrender

In July 1945 a new and fearful force had burst
upon the world. American scientists had completed
an atom bomb. The energy of the atom had been
successfully harnessed for destruction.

The bomb was tested in the New Mexican desert,
and the monstrous explosion proved it to be a
weapon which could end, perhaps by a single stroke,
the widespread and fruitless slaughter of the Pacific
war. The lives of thousands, probably millions, of
Americans, British and Japanese, soon to be cast
away in an invasion of Japan, might be saved.

When the war in Europe was over the Allied
leaders met at Potsdam, near Berlin, to plan the
final victory. Earlier that year Russia had promised
that after the fall of Germany she would join the
United States, Britain and China in the war against
Japan.

Conscious of the grave responsibility which attended the use of the new bomb, President Truman, with the other Allied chiefs, sent an ultimatum to the Japanese Imperial Command on July 26. The ultimatum was set out in clear, decisive terms. It offered the Japanese war lords unconditional surrender as the only alternative to "prompt and utter destruction." Three years and eight months after Pearl Harbor the day of reckoning had come.

Japanese faith in victory was at last beginning to fade. The country was being bombed with systematic regularity. There was an acute shortage of food and gasoline, and with Germany out of the war the whole force of Allied retaliation was turned on Japan.

The Japanese armed forces were being worked up by propaganda to make a "glorious last stand" on the shores of their homeland. Their discipline and reverence for their Emperor never wavered but they saw that the chance of survival was slim.

When the Potsdam warning arrived, opinion in the highest ranks of the Imperial Government was divided. The Emperor and some of his more humane ministers wished to surrender, but the warmongers were determined to fight on.

Meanwhile, in order to spare the lives of helpless civilians, American aircraft dropped millions of leaflets over Japanese cities warning them of impending disaster.

For ten days the Allies waited in vain for signs of surrender.

On August 6 a Super Fortress of the United States

Air Force, flying at thirty thousand feet, dropped the first atomic bomb on the industrial city of Hiroshima. The devastation was complete, and of the three hundred and twenty thousand inhabitants a quarter were killed.

Even then the Japanese Imperial Command made no move. On August 9 a second bomb was dropped, on Nagasaki, with the same effect. On that day Russia invaded Manchuria.

On August 15, for the first time in the history of Japan, the Emperor directly addressed his people. The hundred and twenty-fourth Emperor broke away from the ancestral role of the Son of Heaven, living in sacred isolation, and spoke to them as a man, telling them that they must accept defeat. "We have resolved to pave the way for a grand peace for all the generations to come by enduring the unendurable and suffering what is insufferable."

The war in the Far East was ended. Throughout the United States, on each battle-scarred Pacific island and in every peace-loving land, the news of the invasion of Japan, hanging over every American home, had been miraculously lifted. Peace had come to a war-weary world.

On September 2, 1945, the great battleship *Missouri* lay at anchor in Tokyo Bay. Two Japanese envoys, Mamoru Shigemitsu, representing the Emperor and the government, and Yoshijiro Umezu, representing the Imperial Armed Forces, stiffly climbed the gangway to the flag deck. With inscrutable faces they signed the unconditional surrender of their country.

The Instrument of Surrender was received by General Douglas MacArthur, Supreme Commander for the Allied Powers. With him were Admiral Nimitz and representatives of the other Allied nations.

The Japanese dreams of a Far Eastern Empire had crumbled to dust.

The atomic bombs did not win the war, but they certainly hastened the victory. Japanese defeat was already assured by the mighty industrial power of America and the firm intention of brave men of many nations to fight for freedom.

But it must never be forgotten that, by splitting the atom, men of science have released a gigantic force which will in the future be used either for great good or terrible evil in the service of mankind.

306